ARK
HIVE

a memoir of south louisiana

MARTHE REED

the operating system print//document

ARK HIVE

ISBN: 978-1-946031-47-1
Library of Congress Control Number: 2019902620
copyright © 2018 by Marthe Reed
edited and designed by ELÆ [Lynne DeSilva-Johnson] with Lori Anderson Moseman

is released under a Creative Commons CC-BY-NC-ND (Attribution, Non Commercial, No Derivatives) License:
its reproduction is encouraged for those who otherwise could not afford its purchase in the case of academic, personal, and other creative usage from which no profit will accrue.

Complete rules and restrictions are available at:
http://creativecommons.org/licenses/by-nc-nd/3.0/

For additional questions regarding reproduction, quotation, or to request a pdf for review contact operator@theoperatingsystem.org

This text was set in Freight Neo Pro, Avenir, Minion, and OCR-A Standard.

The cover uses one of Harold Fisk's maps from 1944, a series of studies of the historical traces of the Mississippi river produced for the Army Corps of Engineers.
More at http://www.radicalcartography.net/index.html?fisk

Books from The Operating System are distributed to the trade by Ingram, with additional and small-batch production by Spencer Printing, in Honesdale, PA, in the USA.

The operating system is a member of the **Radical Open Access Collective**, a community of scholar-led, not-for-profit presses, journals and other open access projects. Now consisting of 40 members, we promote a progressive vision for open publishing in the humanities and social sciences.

Learn more at: http://radicaloa.disruptivemedia.org.uk/about/

Your donation makes our publications, platform and programs possible! We <3 You.
bit.ly/growtheoperatingsystem

the operating system

www.theoperatingsystem.org
operator@theoperatingsystem.org

ARK HIVE

ADVANCE PRAISE FOR *ARK HIVE*

"There are locations—like Hawai'i, like Louisiana—where cultures are unique to the place, and outsiders are made to know themselves from insiders. As a poet familiar with issues of appropriation and theft, Marthe Reed asked herself how a Californian who had lived in Providence and Perth, could write about Louisiana, a place she loved over her many years of living in Lafayette. "Writing Louisiana, outsider-inside, poles of affection and alienation push and pull against me." Her answer was to piece together an archive, and to write an epic from its documents: photographs, maps, names of birds, travel journals, histories, languages. What ultimately brings this material to life are the heart-lyrics stitched through the whole: from "threnody": "I keep the contents of my heart / stacked in wet clay / heavy with downpour," where "behind the grate the small / eyes of an armadillo / muted reek / of urine and feces[.]" The threnody she wrote was for a beautiful, fraught, and fragile place. It grieves me to write my paragraph in the past tense. Shortly before she died she told me, "We're all going to die and no one will remember us; it's ok." We are here to remember her and this ravishing, important, necessary work."

—SUSAN M. SCHULTZ

"Here. Now. Live. Marthe Reed's intimate engagement with South Louisiana will moor you to wherever you find yourself. An "act of memory and affection," *ARK HIVE* teaches us how to attend to place. "Following the ley-lines carved out in the streets and bayous of a rapidly eroding landscape, this collection refuses stability, confident of the only riddle and the manifold voices activating it." Reed's hive is a choral fugue of over 85 voices: jazz legends, FEMA officials, fishermen, botanists, bakers, executives, imprisoned citizens, literary icons—neighbors all—knit multiple languages into an exquisite sampler of contemporary poetics. Lush with flora, handmade maps, collaged language and altered documents sing resiliency; this "palimpsest of deluge and silt" flourishes amid debacles—Katrina, BP oil spill, and Texas Brine. A spine of questions borrowed from Bhanu Kapil (the how-what-when of bodily love-n-fear) sutures readers into Reed's tender, monumental dance: "the band is already playing step, slow-quick, quick." Mesmerizing. It is as if she never left Louisiana, as if she never left us."

—LORI ANDERSON MOSEMAN

"Marthe Reed's ecological long poem ARK HIVE is a tour de force, a towering work in the field of documentary poetics that both sounds the alarm with sonic brilliance and subverts its own monumentality through the interrogation of place. ARK HIVE enacts on a formal level the trembling prairie of South Louisiana and so unfolds in a constant state of oscillation: between prose and poetry, fact and uncertainty, the lyric and the visual, English and French, French and Atakapa-Ishak, and, most of all, between celebration of and elegy for the "green bottomland forest, green coastal seas, green marsh grass—prairie tremblant—shifting in the wet." In an extraordinary and personal meditation on one of the most fractured and ecologically vulnerable regions in the known world, Reed writes as an insider-outsider of the umwelt where she lived for eleven years: "Here and not here, what to make of this place called home?" Through arduous research, oral histories, and even hand-drawn maps, ARK HIVE leaves prairie-wide space for the reader to truly consider and understand the impact of racism, corporate malfeasance, and the widening delta of chemical spills on this place and the people who live here. ARK HIVE asks us whether we can survive ourselves—our flooding, our oil industry—and if a new sociality, a new way of being with others, as encapsulated by this book, may help ensure the survival of species, ourselves included."

—HENK ROSSOUW

"It's no wonder that Reed quotes poet C. D. Wright at the start of the work as Wright's work covering south Louisiana could no doubt be seen as a necessary prerequisite to Reed's own project. In the opening pages, Reed approaches her predicament as if she were a researcher placed in a foreign land, situating herself among her surroundings, in the midst of a condition of place that is both physically distant and so very different from the places she had previously lived. From there, she leans into language, the language of water, of floods and earth reclaimed, only to be lost again as the seasons change in places that are far away, the words occasionally scattered across the pages like the silt that drives the Mississippi water to the Gulf of Mexico.

ARK HIVE is the memoir of a person but it is also the narrative of a place, how it came to exist in the time that Reed was living there. We traverse the geography as we traverse the culture, one affected deeply by Hurricane Katrina and also the governmental response to that disaster. Here the language is erased, something that nearly happened somewhere between the storm and the individuals in charge of helping those caught in the middle. The book ends in another crisis — one for her as 'nomadic wanderer' and for the Louisiana coast, changed by the oil spewing from the bottom of the ocean that no one could seemingly stop.

While south Louisiana went through change, so did Marthe, this project tying those changes together, through her own choices of form and thought and language to a kind of self-identification through place, through shared traumas. This was a place once foreign that by the end is reflective of the journey of an individual poet among many who witnessed along with her.

Marthe Reed passed away on April 10th with *ARK HIVE* scheduled as part of The Operating System's 2019 'cohort,' a word choice Marthe would no doubt have loved for its sense of comradery among writers and those who publish them, something she embodied for the rest of us."

—AMISH TRIVEDI, for *Jacket 2*

However briefly I find myself in a strange place, I am intent on locating myself; where I came from at this point is portable; I carry it with me.
—C.D. Wright

the disasters / we place on the tare are weightless
—Jaimie Gusman

TABLE OF CONTENTS

Here and Not — 15

once
under pressure of water — 21
Réponds: Who was responsible for the suffering of your mother? — 22
Displacements/Deformation: Sunrise People — 23
Left behind — 25
Île Copal Sugarcane — 27
Réponds: Where do you come from? — 29
Displacements/Deformation: Sunrise People (2) — 31
topos: an ode — 32
Coulée — 33
Displacements/Deformation: Sunrise People (3) — 34
Water and history (1) — 35
Displacements/Deformation: Sunrise People (4) — 38
water — 39
Réponds: Who are you and whom do you love? — 41

afore
Réponds: How did you arrive? — 48
Ode: negotiation with place — 49
'Tit Ben — 51
When the waters recede — 52
Land and water — 53
threnody — 56
Réponds: What is the shape of your body — 57
Take Me To The River — 58
Réponds: How did you arrive? (2) — 59
Flora — 60
Réponds: What do you remember about the earth? — 61
Réponds: What this means — 63
what Texaco used: Jimmi Martin — 64

thereupon
Lapse :: a city — 70
Plaquemine Aquifer — 72
Report Réponds: What this means (2) — 75
current of geography — 76
Myrtle Grove Trailer Park — 77
Réponds: Whom do you love? — 79

whence
KATRINA — 84

all at once
Barataria Bay — 104
Water and history (2): Macondo Prospect — 106
reel — 111
Réponds: What is the shape of your body? (2) — 112
Lake Martin — 113
Water and history (3) — 114
threnody — 116
Water and history (4): Chandeleur Sound — 117
Clean-up — 118
gulf coast toad — 119

heretofore
Awakening: Grand Isle — 124
Chemical Louisiana — 126
Grand Isle — 127
grand isle: pat landry — 129
erode || erase — 131
Réponds: What are the consequences of silence? — 132
the remembered place — 133
Politics — 135

on that occasion
the old city — 143
les quartiers — 144
Binx's Blues — 145
unnatural metropolis — 151
Vieux Carré — 154
wasted city — 157

by and by
Réponds: Describe a morning you woke without fear — 161
Boat-minded People — 162
blowout: Melvin Lirette — 163
Réponds: Tell me what you know about dismemberment — 164
Stormtracker — 165
Wasted — 168
Mapping — 169
oilfield dreams: roy champagne — 170
Dead Waste — 172
Réponds: How will you live now? — 173

henceforth

Les 'Cadiens	179
threnody	180
Bayou Corne incident	181
Catechism	184
Texas Brine Company, LLC	186
sudden sun	191
threnody	192
Réponds: And what would you say if you could?	193

after-words

Acknowledgements	197
An Active Acknowledgement: Reflections on *Ark Hive* - *Brenda Iijima*	198
Editor's Note: on *ARK HIVE* after Marthe	203
About Marthe Reed	204

HERE AND NOT

I was not there, yet I was there.
—Ernest Gaines, *A Lesson Before Dying*

"Hub City," center of Acadiana and straddling the Vermillion River, Lafayette lies almost due west of New Orleans across the Atchafalaya Basin. The basin, formed by the Mississippi as it laid down successive depositional lobes—Sale-Cypremort, Teche, and Lafourche—the great river switching back and forth finding the shortest route to the Gulf, giving rise to the whole of south Louisiana along the way. If not for the Army Corps of Engineers, its locks and levees, the Mississippi would now enter the Gulf by way of the Atchafalaya Basin and River.

My own route to Lafayette took the long way around: from Western Australia by way of Indiana, by way of San Diego, by way of Providence, Rhode Island, by way of San Diego earlier on, by way of Central California farm, an almond orchard in the countryside near Escalon. Neither here nor there, though here nonetheless: eleven years in Lafayette. When the jet landed in New Orleans, July 2002, stepping outside our eye-glasses immediately fogged up, as when in winter elsewhere we had come in from the cold. Summer humidity in Louisiana does not rest, the evenings no less unrelenting than midday. Tomato plants give up come July, the heat of mid-morning through most of the night sapping their resilience. Wake up, stand outside in the shade, sweat. Summer teaches us to slow down, have a sno-cone: plan to exercise come winter. Here in the wet, green tangles everywhere in summer. Up telephone poles and along the wires, across bridges, through gaps in the asphalt and cracks in the sidewalk (where there are sidewalks, sometimes), wherever earth gathers unbidden in human spaces. No rooting it out. Green. Green verges beside roads and highways, ferns profligate across oaks branches, moss over wood railings, over brick and rendered walls. Green rice fields, green bottomland forest, green coastal seas, green marsh grass—*prairie tremblant*—shifting in the wet.

Being in, though not of this place, by what permission do I write about it, *here* where I live(d)? After school, I listen to the men cutting hair at Ike's Barber Shop, my child sitting high in the red chair listening also. Their talk flows around me, unfathomable, a French I can neither parse nor piece together, though it holds me still listening, as to the sound of water tumbling over root and rock. I overhear folk chatting in Poupart's Bakery, cups clinking against saucers, while I order epi or baguette, the beignets and hand pies calling from the counter. *Français cadien*. Old world French, 17th Century and code-switching French, 'Cadien. Mixed. *Chatoui. Rat du bois. Bequine, plaquemine, rodee. Suce-fleur. Up the bayou. Make the bahdin.* Five million *nutra rats* eating up the coast.

A friend invites us to dinner, her home a circle of rooms leading one into the next. No center, only the circuit: kitchen to living room to bedroom to bedroom to back room to kitchen. Did you miss me? The porch ceiling, painted "haint" blue, hints at sky warding off spirits who cannot cross water—Gullah knowledge carried across the south. Blue ceilings guard against insects also, mosquitos plying the air, owning the evening.

I walk the woods spying for raccoon tracks (chatoui, *cat yes*), armadillo burrows, passerine fliers stopping over. Phoebes, flycatchers, nuthatches, sparrows. I purchase guidebooks for native trees and plants, native birds. In my neighbor's yard, bottle-brush hosts brown thrashers and ruby-throated hummingbirds; I once spotted a Baltimore Oriole, orange-and-black-bodied, among it brushes. Magnolia and live oak line the median of our street. In spring, the astonishing scent and size of magnolia blossoms, their sprawling, creamy tepals circling the green and gold "woman house" (gynoecium) and spikey yellow "man house" (andoceum). Seed-making and germination. Coming to know this place by means of books and my feet, listening: Atchafalaya pronounced uh-CHAF-uh-lie-uh not ATCH-uh-fuh-lie-uh. Puh-CAHN not PEE-can. Sound of squirrel scolds rain from the oak trees, *cher* become *sha*.

Lafayette is Catholic country, a tradition familiar and not, my mother's Episcopalian faith never rooted in me, nor Judaism in my husband. At school, our children navigate the shoals of piety among the faithful, vegetarianism among the carnivorous. Kin-less also, we orbit the edges of extended families upon which community takes form here. Outsiders-in-the-midst. Mike digs in, devouring mounds of boiled crawfish or trays of oysters half-shelled, drenched in garlic and tabasco, washed down with a bottle of LA 31. Oysterloaf in New Orleans, rabbit plate-lunch in Lafayette, hot boudin at the roadside stop. Praising their grandmothers' rice and gravy, dirty rice, or corn maque choux and shrimp, my students gape in disbelief when they discover I do not eat meat or seafood: "But what *do* you eat?" they wonder, amazed. Often Lebanese food, heritage of waves of Maronite immigrants from what would eventually be known as Lebanon. Local eggs, mirlitons, Cajun Country Rice™, roasted chilies and grilled okra, cornbread, collards, Creole tomatoes, muscadines. Sweet corn, sweet corn, sweet corn and peaches. Pickled okra, cheese grits or Zea's sweet corn grits with roasted red pepper coulis. Wild blackberries and pick-your-own blueberries in summer, oranges, Meyer lemons, satsumas in winter.

Writing Louisiana, outsider-inside, poles of affection and alienation push and pull against me. An astonishing and richly diverse region, both culturally and ecologically, its inhabitants have sold paradise for oil and gas money, ignored the most vulnerable, allowed schools, hospitals, and the poor to bear the burden of economic crises, crises often manufactured through taxgiveaways to the affluent and corporations, spending one-time monies as if they would last forever. Paradise is poverty-stricken, imprisoning its citizens at the highest rate in the country: 816/100,000 – far greater than even Russia's 492. Its waters, polluted and poisoned, its coastlines washing away at perilous rates – 2000 square miles in just 80 years. By 2050, if global temperatures rise just two degrees, erosion combined with Antarctic ice melt will reduce New Orleans to an island tied to land by a bridge-cum-highway, the state's coastline a series of slender fingers in the sea: New Iberia, Morgan City, Thibodeaux perched upon the flood.

Still, who am I to rebuke or challenge, to call into question? Is this my place, too, outsiderinside? I lived in south Louisiana eleven years, eleven years in love and in despair. Do those years cede me ground to write? No Cajun, no Creole, no Louisianan by birth or adoption? By what permission? Only love, heart broken open again and again. Sky over New Orleans, that endless expanse of blue and cloud, high and wide as all the earth, or so it seems. Walker Percy had the way of it, "a sketch of cloud in the mild blue sky and the high thin piping of waxwings comes from everywhere." The soft mutterings of the Gulf, water lapping sand or mud, Kate Chopin's "voice of the sea whispering through the reeds that [grow] in the salt water pools," "white clouds suspended idly over the horizon."

The mass of vegetation composing a swamp: Lake Martin's bald cypress, water tupelo, and live oaks draped in Spanish Moss, seeds afloat on the water. Elm, ash, pecan, buttonbush, palmetto. Blue-eyed grass and red buckeye. Invasive bladderwort, water hyacinth, fanwort, coontail, duckweed, and hydrilla tangle the water where native lotus, yellow and blue flag iris, red iris and water hyssop thrive also. Powdery thalia. Sedges all along the lake's margin. The extraordinary population of birds inhabiting the lake: White Ibises, Anhingas, Neotropic Cormorants, Snowy Egrets, Little Blue Herons, Green Herons, Great Egrets, Roseate Spoonbills, Tricolored Herons, Cattle Egrets, Yellow-crowned Night-Herons, Black-crowned Night-Herons, and Great Blue Herons. Common Moorhen and American Coots, Belted Kingfishers. Along the levee trail: Pine and Yellow-throated Warblers, Northern Parula, White-eyed Vireos, and Indigo Buntings; flycatchers, woodpeckers, nuthatches, wrens. In the air and in the woods, Sharpshinned Hawks, Cooper's Hawks, Broad-winged Hawks, Red-tailed Hawks, Barn Owls, Eastern Screech-Owls, Great Horned Owls, Barred Owls, Common Nighthawks. All these species and myriad others, the swamp a-thrum with life.

At Jefferson and East Main Streets, sunset rises over Pat's Diner, saffron and orange tumult of clouds towering. Cajun shaved ice stands: watermelon, raspberry, orange, and pink lemonade or wedding cake, guava, piña colada. Drive-through daiquiri stands where, with a quick bit of tape on the lid, you're good to go. Fishing camps at the coast, hunting camps in the woods. Back yard gardens, back yard chickens: agriculture given way to oil field support. Last Borden's Ice Cream store in the nation. Dance the two-step at Blue Moon Saloon to Feufollet and Lost Bayou Ramblers. Krewes and courirs of Mardi Gras, beads stranded in the limbs of oak trees all year long. Kayak Lake Chicot, Lake Martin, Lake Fausse Pointe. Segregated city, de facto segregated schools: poor and black northside, affluent and white along the river. Meet in the middle? Festivals Acadiens et Créoles, Festival International. In the city, two public access points to the Vermillion, its winding swath obscured by private estates.

Eluding silence, I write amid fragments, from journals, photographs, memory, archives—time capsule of a disintegrating world. A place and an idea impossible to reconstruct, it falls apart in my hands, its multitudes. What are these fragments, this narrative? I build a box of loose pages, maps, stray keys, and seeds. *Memento mori.* What to keep, what to give away? What will not come with me, or might? Here and not here, what to make of this place called home?

An archive is an act of memory and affection, of loss: adrift upon a skim of oil, a scud of cloud, fragments on the floating Gulf.

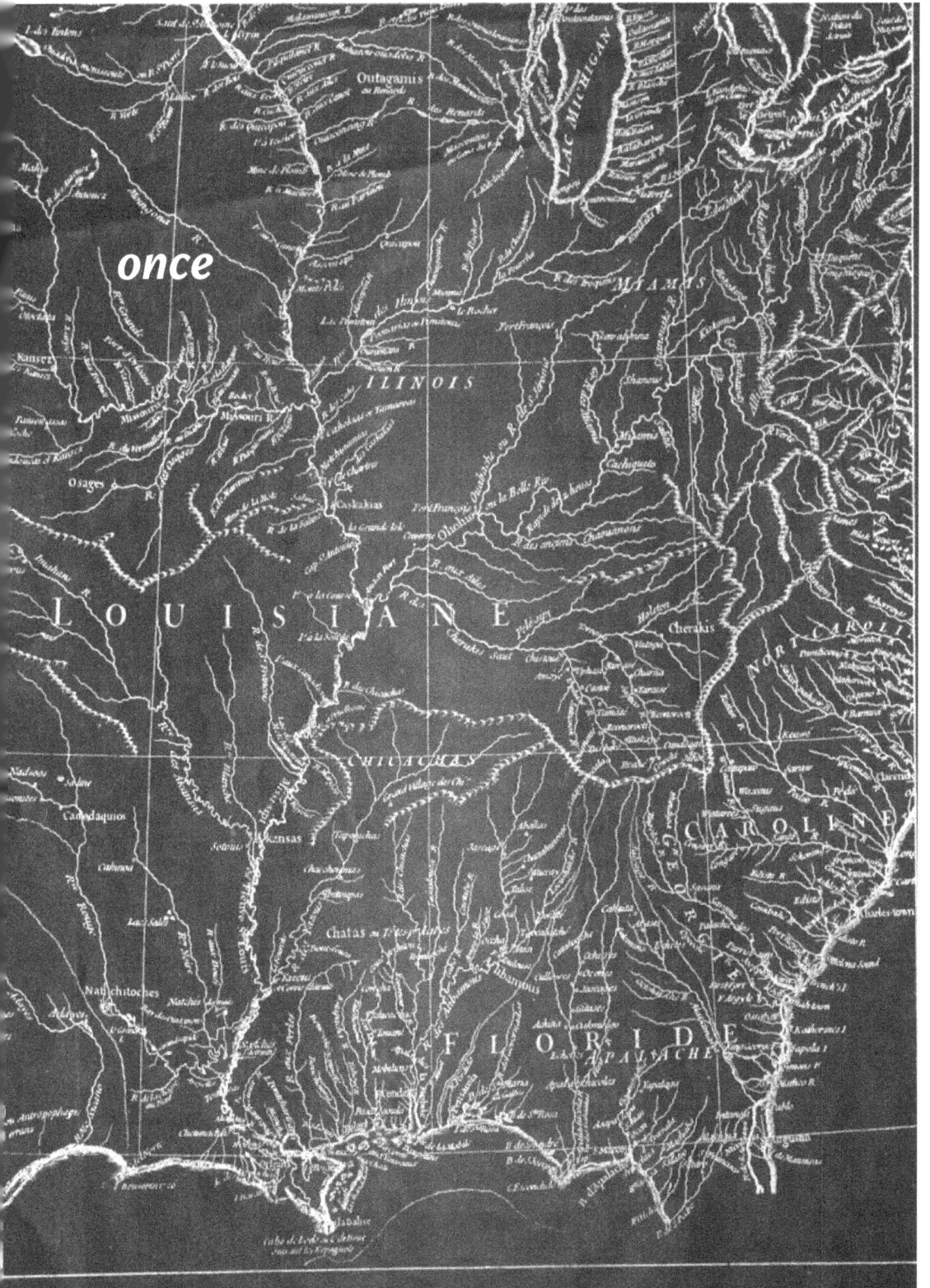

CARTE DE LA LOUISIANE
(Dressée par d'Anville, en 1746).

water under pressure

assume a posture of prayer
or regret

submerged land ::
what holds

in what
            time or water

    pattern
land under

    suspension no
petition

pressure of
((colloidal)) sediment

flood plain
pierced

and patched
            wetland ::

fluvial terrace   marsh
bayou
a subjective

state
decays against a lost

margin of error
registering ruin

((forfeiture))
furrowed

ex
-tracted   ((ex)tent)

    marais ::
        :: marécages

Réponds: Who was responsible for the suffering of your mother?

　　　　each to

　　　　　　　　　　each

　　the switch

　　　　　　already in my hand

　　　　　　　　　　　　a large round
　　　　　　　　　　　　fixed on a
　　　　　　　　　　　　pyramidal knob

　　　　　　a strong smell
　　　　　　a burning taste
　　　　　　delicate
　　　　　　　　to feel indisposed

Displacements/Deformation: [1] Sunrise People

I will wait for you to come
you to come

the Mothers
(from) below

here, in time, soon

'nya'-uta
'no'kne

hukē't
ne'

ō'l

        in the sands
        on the banks along the woods

        in the red soil
        in the pine-barrens
        on the high hills

[1] Atakapa-Ishak words and phrases and rough English translations from *A Dictionary of Atakapa Language* accompanied by texts.

The forest we were then in was thick enough so that none of my men could be seen. I formed them into three detachments, and arranged them in such a way as to surround these savages, and to leave them no way of retreat except by the pond. I then made them all move forward, and I sent ahead a subordinate chief to ascertain what nation these savages belonged to, and what would be their intentions toward us. We were soon assured that they were Atakapas, who, as soon as they saw us, far from seeking to defend themselves, made us signs of peace and friendship. There were one hundred and eighty [180] of them of both sexes, busy, as we suspected, smoke-drying meat. As soon as my three detachments had emerged from the forest, I saw one of these savages coming straight toward me: at first sight, I recognized that he did not belong to the Atakapas nation; he addressed me politely and in an easy manner, unusual among these savages. He offered food and drink for my warriors which I accepted, while expressing to him my gratitude. Meat was served to my entire detachment; and during the time of about six hours that I remained with this man, I learned that he was a European; that he had been a Jesuit; and that having gone into Mexico, these people had chosen him as their chief. He spoke French rather well. He told me that his name was Joseph; but I did not learn from what part of Europe he came.

He informed me that the name Atakapas, which means eaters of men, had been given to this nation by the Spaniards because every time they caught one of them, they would roast him alive, but that they did not eat them; that they acted in this way toward this nation to avenge their ancestors for the torture that they made them endure when they had come to take possession of Mexico; that if some Englishmen or Frenchmen happened to be lost in this bay region, the Atakapas welcomed them with kindness, would give them hospitality; and if they did not wish to remain with them they had them taken to the Akancas, from where they could easily go to New Orleans.

He told me: "You see here about one-half of the Atakapas Nation; the other half is farther on. We are in the habit of dividing ourselves into two or three groups in order to follow the buffalo, which in the spring go back into the west, and in autumn come down into these parts; there are herds of these buffalo, which go sometimes as far as the Missouri; we kill them with arrows; our young hunters are very skilful at this hunting. You understand, moreover, that these animals are in very great numbers, and as tame as if they were raised on a farm; consequently, we are very careful never to frighten them. When they stay on a prairie or in a forest, we camp near them in order to accustom them to seeing us, and we follow all their wanderings so that they cannot get away from us. We use their meat for food and their skins for clothing. I have been living with these people for about eleven years; I am happy and satisfied here, and have not the least desire to return to Europe. I have six children whom I love a great deal, and with whom I want to end my days. When my warriors were rested and refreshed, I took leave of Joseph and of the Atakapas, while assuring them of my desire to be able to make some returns for their friendlywelcome, and I resumed my Journey.

— Louis LeClerc Milfort, 1781

Left Behind

Russet and gray, thick as locusts, "the birds poured in in countless multitudes." Voracious migrants "wandering about," eating, consuming everything, beechnuts, acorns, chestnuts. Blueberries, grapes, cherries, mulberries, poke berries, the fruit of dogwoods. Earthworms, caterpillars, snails (in breeding season), wandering multitudes, "passing in undiminished numbers....three days in succession." Three days in succession. Tens of thousands at a time *darkening the sky*. *Passager*, "Obscured as by an eclipse," like the sound of thunder approaching. Cheap meat for slaves and the poor. Extinct.[2]

Greeny-blue *periquito*, cream-capped "little" "wig". Parrot, parakeet, twelve to thirteen inches long, wild orange eyespot and blue. Blue-bodied Louisiana long-tailed conure. Cone tail. Noisy, nesting in tree hollows, cypress and sycamore. Bottomland parrot, swamp parrot voraciously sampling orchards and vines: thieves, raiders, robbers. *Kelinky* among the Chickasaw, their flesh poisoned cats. Painted by Audubon, greeny-blue and cream-capped carcasses. *Periquito*. Women's hats, deforestation. Extinct.

Slender with a slight and downward. Warbler, possessing a slightly downward curving beak. Some certain, in earlier times, along the Lower Suwannee. Slender olive-green passerine with yellow lores, yellow abdomen. Yellow-bellied Bachman amid swampy blackberry and cane thickets, *Zeep-* (the millinery trade) *-zzzzzip*. Warbler, "sparrow" "shaped" *Passeriformes*. Yellow shoulder patch and bright rump. Black and gray and olive-gray. "A lively active bird," males more vivid than their mates, "seizing insects from the air."[3] In low-lying wet forests: oaks, hickories, black gums. Lost breeding and wintering habitat, last seen (hats and haberdashery) 1988. A severe decline. Extinct.

Blue-backed and red-capped giant, shiny black giant amid woods. White upper and lower wing trailing: Grail Bird, Lord God Bird. And black. Red capped, red crowned emperor of the Singer Tract, Madison Parish, Louisiana. Last Southern primeval forest tract. Logging tract, forest cut to oblivion, Chicago Mill and Lumber Company. Board feet better than Lord God (Bird). Godbird. By spring 1944, a single female Ivory-bill found in a small stand of uncut timber, adrift in devastation: last verified sighting. Grail bird. Critically imperiled, extinct in Louisiana. Lord God. Definitely, or probably, extinct.

Curlew, a clear "target of choice," thousands at one time, among market hunters after extirpating the passenger pigeon. A twenty-year assault, thousands killed at a time, pursued autumn and spring, migrant fliers traversing the globe in long elliptical arcs. A clear whistling call. Eskimo Curlews, shorebirds: migrating from high arctic tundra to Tierra del Fuego. Lost tallgrass prairie, migratory insect hunters. Lost pasturage, lost Rocky Mountain grasshoppers, grasshopper forage. Fields, pastures, dry edges of marshes, vegetated dunes. Whatever remains. Browny-green or blue eggs. Mottled brown and white throated birds. "formerly part of the established biota, possibly still persisting..." Not seen for thirty years. Not seen. Almost certainly extinct.

White with red crown, red patch along cheeks and down, black wing-tips, long dark legs. Wetlands, marshes, mudflats, wet prairies, and fields. Their bugling whooping sound or cry. Unison call of crane pairs, waking at dawn. One to three eggs, blotchy olive-colored eggs, one juvenile. One white and cinnamon-brown juvenile. Decimated by habitat loss and hunting. 1941: 21 wild, two captive birds. 2011: 437 wild, 165 captive. One of only two native North American crane species, *Grus Americana*. Endangered in Louisiana. Reestablished in White Lakes Wetlands Conservation Area, 47 birds. 47 birds. Critically imperiled.

[2] Quotes from James John Audubon.

[3] Audubon quoting Rev. John Bachman, who sent the painter specimens, even though "having only procured a few specimens of both sexes, without being able to find a nest". (*Ornithilogical Biography*, vol ii, page 483, both)

Île Copal Sugarcane

I linger over a bowl of lemon sorbet, downtown Lafayette hot and bright in midday sun. Across the street, Confederate General Alfred Mouton, cross-armed and stern, stares back. His papaw's Île Copal Plantation founded the city. One hundred and twenty enslaved people's labor paid for his father's Georgetown College education, secured the family's wealth. Later JeanJacques-Alfred-Alexandre Mouton was sent to West Point, though he knew little English. After a brief commission, he resigned and took up sugarcane growing, that is, until the outbreak of the Civil War. Donated by the United Daughters of the Confederacy in 1920, in honor of his valor for "The Cause," enfranchising Jim Crow, the statue stands, with its back to Lee Avenue, facing Jefferson Street before the former town hall. The way history asserts itself everywhere.

Adjacent to downtown, the Freetown-Port Rico neighborhood takes its name both for the Free People of Color and freed people of Reconstruction-era Lafayette who took up residence in "Mouton Addition"—a subdivision of the plantation established by his father, Alexander Mouton—and for the variety of sugarcane grown at Île Copal, a Caribbean import.

A plantation of 19,000 acres along the Vermilion River, Île Copal's sugar production made the Moutons both very wealthy and powerful. Though local lore holds that the Acadians were never slave holders, Jean Mouton, the founder of the sugar plantation, was born in Acadie and expulsed by the British along with his brother Marin and the rest of the Acadians. Nor was Mouton alone in enslaving people: Acadians Isadore Broussard, Honoré Beraud, Charles Trahan, Andrew Martin, Claude Martin, and Antoine Mouton all depended on the labor of enslaved people to work their plantations. Île Copal eventually came into the hands of Jean Mouton's son Alexander, who would become a U.S. Senator, Governor of Louisiana and, in 1861, convener of the Louisiana Secession Convention.

On April 17, 1863, charged with defending his hometown, General Mouton retreated across the Pinhook Bridge, burning it to stop the Union advance, and fleeing on to Opelousas where Union forces eventually caught up with him. Though not before Union General Nathaniel Banks captured Île Copal, arrested Governor Mouton, burnt his sugar mill, sent him to prison in New Orleans, and liberated the 120 enslaved people held there. Île Copal became General Banks' headquarters. The following year, Brigadier General Alfred Mouton was mortally wounded at the Battle of Mansfield by a marksman in Banks' army. Mouton's cavalry "With tears of grief and rage in their eyes….ran on through the deadly hail, determined to avenge the death of their leader,"[4] losing a full third of their number in the ensuing battle. Language proffers "valor", dressing up white supremacy's evil.

As for the statue, at the threat of a 1980 lawsuit from the venerable Daughters, the city agreed to a permanent injunction, promising not to move it. A local group "Why Not Alfred?", advocating for keeping the statue, demands no new "political correctness verbiage" be attached to "our community heritage": a man who died

---

[4] John D. Winter, Civil War in Louisiana.

defending the Confederacy. What next, they wonder, give up streets named for famous Confederates?

Apparently, the names—lost, erased, forgotten—of those enslaved at Île Copal offer no such succor to either community or heritage, the names of those enslaved at Walnut Grove, Myrtle Plantation, and Long Plantation. Nor does the question of the distribution of the wealth, generated by black lives for which no return has ever been made, arise: forty acres and a mule sacrificed to wage labor, share-cropping, Jim-Crow, entrenched poverty. The three lowest performing schools in Lafayette Parish in 2015 are majority black: N. P. Moss Preparatory (76%), Lafayette Middle (80%), and Alice Boucher Elementary (96%). Yet African Americans account for only 26% of the parish's population. The way the past inflicts its violence on the future, again and again, rending apart "society, fellowship, friendly intercourse."

Réponds: Where do you come from?

how far back?
Australia the coasts Indiana ||||Canada Illinois Virginia Arkansas || California || California || California || Britain and Ireland Britain's Ireland || Africa || Asia || any elsewhere

no || where

further back?
the mountains || Rockies and Appalachians || bread basket Great Plains || Pleistocene silt inland seas || Mississippi River Mississippi River || Mississippi mud-sprawl-swamp subsidence

wet dry wet soaked

here
live oak and water oak bald cypress || tupelo gum || fresh marsh brackish marsh salt || willow-sedge-mangrove || ancient chênières || here || forest and swamp

quaking land

here
mockingbirds cardinals jays sparrows || urban neighbors yardbirds yardbirds yardbirds || (the blues) swamp fiddles porch songs || shade and green || shadeandgreen || interminable || wet

heat

here
Natchez Houma Chitimacha || Choctaw Caddo || Tunica || Atakapas ((Atakapas)) Ishak ||

Atakapas woman and man after death
                        face covered over

Ta'kapa kic n ichā'k ka-ukin, īt utska-ukulat

here

Les Acadiens Acadiennes || Les Cajuns et Créoles "free creoles of color" || Les Créoles du Carib || Code Noir || Code || Noir || black folk || black folk African and French (((white))) || Iberian German Croats et les Chinois || Mexican Vietnamese Lao Filipino Hmong

among

here
memanythingspeople || ((no
one thing

much

Displacements/Deformation: [5] Sunrise People (2)

that is all	lya' něk mōn
there she lived she is	ya' nā kētnat
buried and lies there	imō' cti
I knew her once	(h)ui' xts tanu' kip

to tell about things	cakwa' nts cok
long ago	ku' ltan
she sang	cakyo'kat
her daughter her	ha' ickici'l ha' nīl
grandchild the same	oktanu'k
first, previously	ha'hu
yellow fever	icla'uk
they buried her	imo' culat

she came	mo'hat
my mother	wi okē't
the lake	tu'l
made us grow up	icitsiu'tsicat
we were glad	icatsi cki'ñcat
we did not want to remain	icōñcat kē'tne

[5] Atakapa-Ishak words and phrases and rough English translations from *A Dictionary of Atakapa Language* accompanied by texts.

topos: an ode

black and white cattle
graze amid

cypress
and water oak

among darker
long-leafed pines

I come for wild
phloxes

orchids a narrow
bayou

counterpoint
to my eroding

sense of time
the space

my body makes
in fragmented

course toward
the treeline

in French re-
connaissance

means both
recognition

and gratitude
star grass

and wild aster
whisper about my feet

cartography
of a vanishing world

Coulée

West Bayou Parkway, a suburban road wandering through one high-end suburb toward another, takes its name from the Vermillion River bending along the edge of Lafayette's affluent core. Live oaks over graceful lawns. Manicured gardens green with azaleas, daylilies, roses. Exotic palms in place of palmettos and zamias. The swooping curves of driveways mirror the parkway's meander. At the western terminus of the road, Coulée Mine winds away from the road's margin toward the river, carrying storm water away from the street. Lined with water oaks, tall grasses, overgrowth, the coulée drains directly into the Vermillion, muddy-red river.

Only a month in town, we shelter from the late sun's glare, traveling by way of the shade of the tree-lined street. As we slow down approaching the signal, a vehicle in front of us pauses for the light. The passenger door opens, an arm reaching down to set an emptied McDonald's drink cup onto the asphalt, before the car pulls away, door clicking closed as it glides through the turn. Class warfare?

"Any coulee that's going to be carrying water is going to be carrying trash....When that water's moving, it's like a trash train from the city."

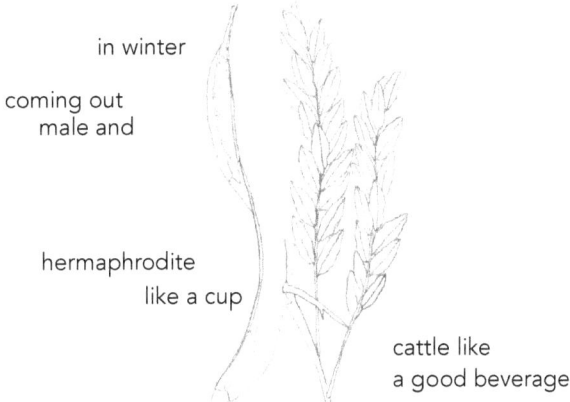

in winter

coming out
male and

hermaphrodite
like a cup

cattle like
a good beverage

Displacements/Deformation: [6] Sunrise People

    on a horse   tsanu'ki
    well with you   nto'l
    a hog goes crying   wān-haihaickit

    in the fire   kidso' nkckin
    we will bake   cakwāktikit
    it out   hita' uc

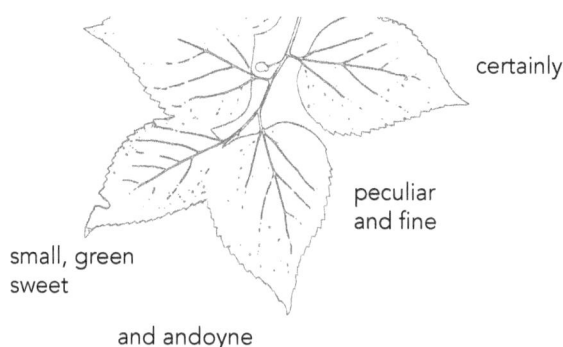

                                         certainly

                                 peculiar
                                 and fine
    small, green
    sweet
            and andoyne

---

[6] Atakapa-Ishak words and phrases and rough English translations from *A Dictionary of Atakapa Language* accompanied by texts.

Water and history (1)

Off to one side of the town was the dwelling place of the Curaca (chief). It was situated on a high mound which now served as a fortress. Only by means of two stairways could one ascend to this house...... beholding the pillage and seizure of his vassals, he grasped a battle-ax and began to descend the stairs with the greatest fury, in the meantime vowing loudly and fiercely to slay anyone who came into his land without permission.
          —Hernando de Soto

accretion
or precipitation
          ((silt   mud
                mangrove roots))

delimits memory
Houma Natchez Caddo Tunica Coushatta

the purposive
organism et le Grand Dérangement
hunters farmers oysterers
loaded on ships and sent

south

         east

Treaty of Utrecht
(Acadie)
involuntary transportation recapitulates
erosion   basin and range

dolomite argillite sandstone to speak of a life

between the 40 th and 49 th parallels
Les Maritimes
wet earth ::   houses
not more than

one room and an attic
rendered moss   and mud   en la louisiane

what remains after flood
two ends of an experiential continuum

dis-
placement the
prerogative of empire
neither rock nor sand

depositional
sedimentary ::
12,000, 15,000 y.a.
migration over a landbridge

green mounds winged serpents thunder
gods   abandoned

Chenco discs stone rolled
across hard clay plazas ||
a progression of attitudes toward the land
|| maize stored in granaries

ways of knowing
earth   hearth   home

locating a sense of place
subjective || states
Atakapa-Ishak Choctaw Chitimacha
Houma

((les Acadiens venus par bateau)
scattered in houses along Happy

Jack Canal
stimuli as sign ((drowned
trees wet land

Emerald Mound's pentagonal
plateau   green

sister mounds abandoned
de Soto's
aftermath
a practice of

intermarriage   alcohol   disease
edging the marginal deltaic

basin
ancient sedimentary cheniers
1600 Acadiens left France for Louisiana
11,500 imprisoned deported drowned disease

oysterers fur trappers marginal
gardeners

Joseph Broussard (dit *beausoleil*)
seining the bayous
failed Mik'maq confederacy
sunlight

"Acadians of the Atakapas" ::
a faculty for exploitation

organic muck
       trans

               sect ll trans

                        act

naviguèrent en pirogues
le long du Golfe

Displacements/Deformation: [7] Sunrise People (4)

    sweet persimmons small grapes,   ōl a'yip
    large grapes   a'liñ hicōm, a'liñ
        hicka'm

    they prayed standing   tawatwe'năt
    sun at the rising   hiye'kiti
    to Otsotat   Utsuta't ut

    they painted themselves with red   hatiu'lco 'n'o'hik
    paint they painted themselves   cakatko'pcěn
    white   hatmē'lco
    they painted themselves black

        na'-u
    feathers   tikpum ne'kin
    at the dancing place

        wā'ci a

    old here

        hiya'ñ Cuka-kulĕt

    yonder they dance

---

[7] Atakapa-Ishak words and phrases and rough English translations from *A Dictionary of Atakapa Language* accompanied by texts. Atakapa-Ishak is no longer a living language.

water

> *All is open.*
> *Open water. Open I.*
> —Muriel Rukeyser, "The Outer Banks"

Open   I
    (eye)

awaiting a predicate
the necessary state

            of departure
    or initial energy

        open water
   open   air

            pitch and

        yaw

              cordgrass

    ((shift
    -ing

       particles of air

   sunonwater

  s   u   n   o   n   w   a   t   e   r

green

  -ing furrow / fallow
        blue echo

   rocking here

                        ((my)) weight over a low
                            dock

                bob
            -bing into green

    horizon
    no edge ::

                                                    rigs hunker on
                                                concrete piers above

                                ((blue))

            fiftyyearold
                    pipelines

                                        crudeoozingintosilt

            w i d e n i n g
                        blue channel

                                                    trammel

                -ed spartina grass

                            saltmarsh ((gnawn
                        prairie a(s)way

Réponds: Who are you and whom do you love?

      an oak a floodplain nothingdry

the rate of compression of memory against

     widows weeds
     an influx of salt

                   4000 miles of river
   or a color   ll g r e e n ll

      damp writes itself into wood   sprawls
         a whole-

duckweed   hyacinth   kudzu
                     noendtoit

      family of pernicious weeds

        hurricane

                              tornado

        flood

    any coastline lined in platforms
    propagates

e   r   o   s   i   o   n

erasure presupposes

                  ((vested) interests

what, love, are you

         EXCESS   nitrogen

        Native
        New Iberian
        Bourbon
        Acadien
        Creole
        West   African

histories (several)
    arrive again and again
    how we

    account for weather
    a kind in
    folly   lost

            languages
        love

    In Atakapas   *widow*   (   )

            water   *had none*

afore

Art. 33.
L'esclave qui aura frappé son maître, sa maîtresse ou le mari de sa maîtresse, ou leurs enfants avec contusion ou effusion de sang, ou au visage, sera puni de mort.

Art. 34.
Et quant aux excès et voies de fait qui seront commis par les esclaves contre les personnes libres, voulons qu'ils soient sévèrement punis, même de mort, s'il y échet.

Aunt Cheyney was jus' out of bed with a sucklin' baby one time, and she run away. Some say that was 'nother baby of massa's breedin'. She don't come to the house to nurse her baby, so they misses her and old Solomon gits the hounds and takes her trail. They gits near her and she grabs a limb and tries to h[o]ist herself in a tree, but them dogs grab her and pull her down. The men hollers them onto her, and the dogs tore her nake[d] and et the breasts plumb off her body. She got well and lived to be a old woman, but 'nother woman has to suck her baby and she ain't got no sign of breasts no more.

> — Narrative of Mary Reynolds, *Enslaved in Louisiana*,
> ca. 1832-1865 Interview conducted ca. 1937,
> Dallas, Texas Federal Writers' Project, WPA

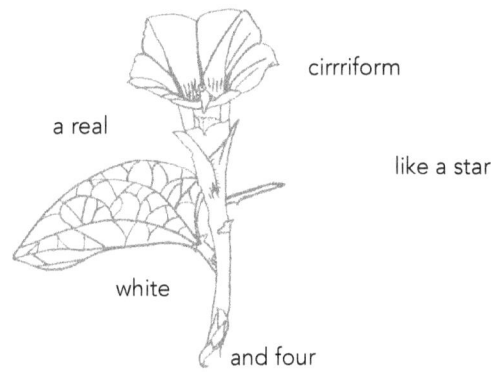

a real

cirrriform

like a star

white

and four

Réponds: How did you arrive?

landbridge-bayou-sea
air

par bateau
et dans le Golfe du Mexique

belly of the slave ship
in the midst of kin

hungry

alone

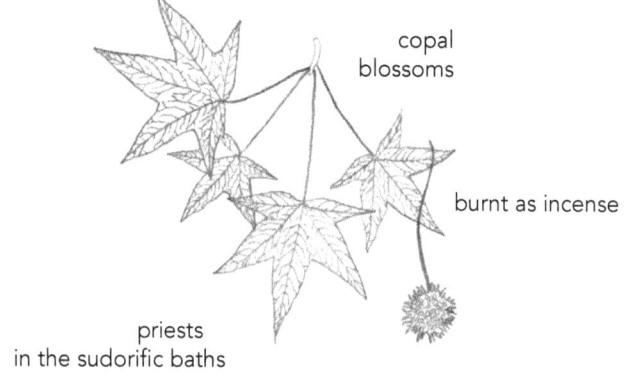

Ode: negotiation with place

                      to articulate a means of entry
                      consensual knife-edged opening
           a sanction against trespass
           Atchafalaya waterway
      silt and flood, bayou slips
      imperceptible over cypress knees
from Choctaw, *bayuk*
a removed people
        a net of language left
        in absence
            swamp lilies and bald cypress
            salt domes, water moccasins, sticky clay
                a sensation or impression of
                humidity, implacable, sprawling Mississippi

    complex branched
    chronicle :: memory and place
        forest and booted feet carry me here
        sweat clinging to my brow, mosquitoes
            drone in the thick air, matted verdure
            palimpsestic language and history—
                damp, bird-foot, opossum, batture
                a translation, articulating experience
            one into an(other)
            place, Mound
      Builders, slavers, French
    colony the wet
whispers its own arguments
over my skin, irrefutable

    topos the relation between
    local particulars and
        human inhabitants
        a world defined by language
            Teche Arcady   Natchez
            Pontchartrain   Tangipahoa
                its surfaces collaborate
                hybrid, synthetic
          Ardoin, Fontenot, Abshire, Segura
          Tchoupitoulas   water oak and
    woodcocks, M. de Iberville, War of 1812
    tupelo gum, zydeco, crawfish, *frottoir*
Army Corps of Engineers
arbitrary and infinite intersections

Suburban topos: live oaks
sheltering houses, loosening foundations—
      abandon leaves and leaf-out all at once
        leaf-litter clattering over the lawn
            lithe green anoles spring, take
            cover under sprawling
                  limbs of purple and white
                    azaleas, waxy camellia leaves
          near natives, these domesticated spawn
        cat, gray intruder, grasped
    solidly in seven-year-old arms
    and borne away, cat and child place

'Tit Ben

Eleven years in south Louisiana does not teach me to eat oysters, crawfish, etouffé. We make vegetarian gumbo only once, and stop, though I adopt "Come see" for the children, learn to accept "How are you, Boo?" from the nurse, recognize my elderly neighbor, youngest of twelve children, as 'Tit Ben. Forbidden French in school, his siblings taught him English so he wouldn't be punished. Never learned his mother tongue.

Bells of St. John's— Église de Saint Jean, once upon a time—peal Sunday mornings over our house tops, a church built on gifted plantation land, Jean Mouton's Île Copal. On the north side of town, the Immaculate Heart of Mary was founded in 1934 to afford positions for four African American priests newly ordained at St. Louis Bay, Mississippi. Immaculate segregation.

Beneath St. Jean's bells, I ignore the heat, plant roses, yellow and white Lady Banksias, Gamecock iris, blue and yellow flags. Weeds pernicious in summer, like the squirrels 'Tit Ben shoots with a BB gun from his porch, thieving his "Japanese plums" and pecans. Across the way, a red tail hawk stoops through live oaks, and flies up clutching a luckless squirrel in its talons, and vanishes into the canopy.

Zamia palms coat their cinnabar seed pods in tawny felt. I mean to collect these but forget. The children trail home strands of Spanish moss from every walk. Swallowtail 'orange dogs' in spring, on the leaves of lemon and orange trees, put away green fat beneath glossy leaves. Later rain clatters over oyster shells, remnants of a solitary feast, yellow flags in the pond flowering.

Locals say Meche's makes the best King Cake, though we prefer Poupart's old Northern Frenchstyle cakes, *galette des rois*, puff pastry filled with frangipane. Sundays we can't buy alcohol until after noon, when church lets out. Red beans and rice, red beans and rice, old chicken gravy and rice.

'Tit Ben chastises us for paying Thomas, the man he recommended to help in our garden, what was asked, rather than what Ben prescribed. Ben promises to report Thomas to his mother. Black indigency and White paternalism, earth-floored "quarters" and neo-classical porch columns.

When the waters recede

*Is there here
a boat's mast claiming my lonely night too?*
—Rickey Laurentiis

TEN DOLLARS REWARD Runaway from the subscriber the day before yesterday, the negress **MELITTE**, aged 24 years, very tall and thin, walks very fast, has lost her front teeth; speaks French and English, and is well known in the city. The Above reward will be paid to whoever will lodge her in jail, and give information thereof at the office of the Courier. Captains of vesse's and all other persons are cautioned against harboring or employing said negresse, as the law will be rigorously enforced against all so offending. June 30. J. A. BONNEVAL.

$50 REWARD I will give the above reward for the apprehension and delivery to me, in Shreveport, LA., of my negro man **LUNN** , who absented himself about the 28 th June last. Lunn is a carpenter by trade, 27 or 28 years of age, weighs about 165 or 170 pounds; he is about six feet height, of dark color, rather slow to speak, but quite plausible in conversation, and of quick motion. The kind of clothing he has on is not recollected. He has a wife at Mr. Wm. Speils, near Keachie, in DeSoto parish, where he has been lately seen. If he is lodged in any jail out of Caddo parish and due notice thereof given and he is delivered to me, I will pay a reward of twenty-five dollars. July 15, 1857. SAM VAN BIBBER.

ONE HUNDRED DOLLARS REWARD Absconded on the 1 ST of March, instant the slave man **CHARLES**, about 28 years old, of brown color, is rather slender and good looking, and keeps his hair well combed, is very polite to well dressed person, has plenty of clothing, he can read and write, speaks French and English, and is about 5 feet 10 inches in height. He came to New Orleans from Maryland above 14 years ago, having belonged to the family of Sherwoods, of St Mary's country, MD. He is supposed to have left on board of some steamboat for the West. I will give $100 reward if taken out of this State, and $50 if taken in this State and returned to me. CHAS. H. TANEY.

TEN DOLLARS REWARD On the 7 th inst, went away a Negro, a baker named **NARCI**, belonging to the nunnery. Those who will bring him to their agent, Antoine Abat, will receive the above Reward. July 26, 1809. URSULINE CONVENT

Land and water

"No page is ever truly blank"
—Craig Santos Perez, *Saina*

something else
obtains inexplicably

another luminosity
between 2 bends in the Mississippi
     (accretion erosion)

a map or mapping
    the visible rend

white ibises   herons   egrets
Dow Chemical churns out polyethylene and methylcellulose

      ((milk jugs and
      milkshakes

wastestream emptying
((dioxin
into the Mississippi

vinyl chloride
a dead
((PVC
zone 1989 Morrisonville
cancer

alley "freetown" freed
((liberated
by Dow))
men and women bought
out and
moved away

de-
populated by Dow

new town
new burial ground

Dow's sprawling 1,400 acre
grounds
PCBs   hexachlorobenzene   dioxin

produced in
Louisiana and Texas
"confined to low-
      income African American communities"

disposal incinerators ((likewise
located))
town wells poisoned
      (air)
   poisoned
abandoned

80 mile long
chemical corridor
Baton Rouge à New Orleans

a field aligned with

      supplication
      rushing water

      flight

any projected (pejorative) "field"   (of endeavor
poisoned

      :: refinery jobs a whole
economy of exploitation

      between river and basin ((Atchafalaya
(((atchafalaya

      geography's bones   surfacing
less and less

                                      steady

              this
                      blank(ed) perspective
history's (   )

coastline

                                                      ((terra incognita

                    sun
                                  ((terra nullius

                                                            glistening

threnody

knowing how this will end
such an awkward alliance
an ache that is not pain
magnolia sweet

raising the levees again and again
shelling boiled peanuts
bowing a fiddle
getting there all along

amid the soak and flow
a good *life*
up and down the coast
barges and rigs

oilfields
gambling on spring and summer
drilled that hole, toolpushing
and quit come trapping season

boat in the water
boat in the water

it gets away from you
this senseless   thrashing

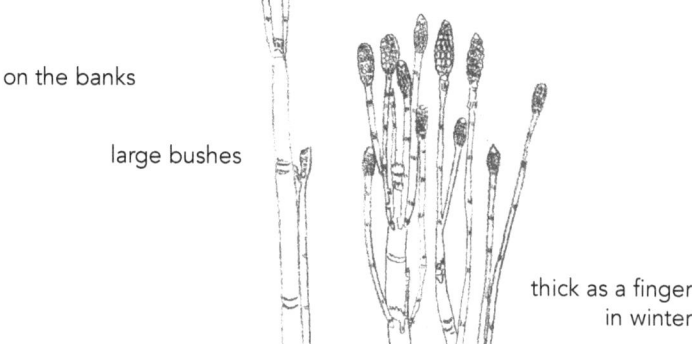

on the banks

large bushes

thick as a finger
in winter

Réponds: What is the shape of your body[8]

Etienne (Neptune)	insurrection	found guilty, hung, and exposed
Garret, Daniel	insurrection	found guilty and hung
Hector	insurrection	found guilty, hung, and exposed
Louis	insurrection	found guilty, hung, and exposed
Jessamin	insurrection	found guilty, hung, and exposed
Theodore	insurrection	found guilty, but recommend mercy
Gilbert	insurrection	guilty, but shot, not hung and exposed
Caesar	insurrection	found guilty, hung, and exposed
Atys	insurrection	found guilty, hung, and exposed
Orphee	insurrection	found guilty, death sentence commuted due to special circumstances
Isaac or Jacques,	insurrection	found guilty, hung, and exposed
Honore	insurrection	found guilty, hung, and exposed
Joseph	insurrection	found guilty, hung, and exposed
Charles	insurrection	hung, but buried (not exposed) because of brother-in-law's acts
Lindor	insurrection	found guilty, hung, and exposed

---

[8] German Coast Uprising: facsimile of original Criminal case 229: 1812, Honore, insurrection. Found guilty, hung, and exposed.

Take Me To The River

> *We the people of New Orleans demand that the Mayor and City Council take immediate action to remove all monuments, school names and street signs dedicated to White Supremacists. These structures litter our city with visual reminders of the horrid legacy of slavery that terrorized so many of this city's ancestors. They misrepresent our community. We demand the freedom to live in a city where we are not forced to pay taxes for the maintenance of public symbols that demean us and psychologically terrorize us. We demand:*
>
> 1. *That the city release a timeline for the immediate removal of the monuments;*
> 2. *That the city expand the definition from 4 specific monuments to encompass all monuments to White Supremacy;*
> 3. *That the city develop a community driven process for the removal of the monuments and the choosing of their replacements.*

Founded in response to the 2015 murders of nine members of the Mother Emmanuel African Methodist Episcopal Church by a white supremacist and the activist Bree Newsome's subsequent removal of the Confederate flag from the South Carolina statehouse grounds, Founded in response to the 2015 murders of nine members of the Mother Emmanuel African Methodist Episcopal Church by a white supremacist and the activist Bree Newsome's subsequent removal of the Confederate flag from the South Carolina statehouse grounds, #TakeEmDownNola[9] pressured the New Orleans community to remove all Confederate monuments in New Orleans, Jim Crow installations re-consecrating the city to the white supremacy of pre-Civil War Louisiana. Mayor Mitch Landrieu and the city council voted to remove four of the twenty statues and committed the community to renaming hundreds of street names and thirty city schools, as well. In May 2017, the fourth statue, Robert E. Lee of Lee Circle, was pulled down. The workers were forced to wear bullet-proof vests and operate the cranes by night to avoid the violence of white supremacist agitators. Of the remaining sixteen monuments, no word.

"the whole history of white supremacist organizations in the South has been one of terrorism." Martin Suber, co-founder #TakeEmDownNola[10] pressured the New Orleans community to remove all Confederate monuments in New Orleans, Jim Crow installations re-consecrating the city to the white supremacy of pre-Civil War Louisiana. Mayor Mitch Landrieu and the city council voted to remove four of the twenty statues and committed the community to renaming hundreds of street names and thirty city schools, as well. In May 2017, the fourth statue, Robert E. Lee of Lee Circle, was pulled down. The workers were forced to wear bullet-proof vests and operate the cranes by night to avoid the violence of white supremacist agitators. Of the remaining sixteen monuments, no word.

---

[9] http://takeemdownnola.org/
[10] https://www.democracynow/2017/5/23/as_;ast_confederate_statue_is_removed

Réponds: How did you arrive? (2)

a series of
steps or decelerating
progressions pas de (no

schematic
covering the familiar
scape ((escape

presupposes return
the past

"an ideal dimension"
or velocity
((water))
aground

              water

always returning
though never fully
retrievable

an archive of lost things
memory
longing grief
ark

hive

      Isle(s)

            Dernière(s)

Flora

Some days I stand at a drawing table, sketching native plants, some rare, some common. Bluevine milkweed, or swallow-wort, twines gorgeously up fence posts, along roadsides, stitches its way through fields. Some call it a noxious weed though the monarchs love them. How not love something named "honeyvine" with its heart-shaped leaves? Its lines, simple and diffuse, come easily to the page. Equisetum hyemale, on the other hand, demands my attention, its creamy strobilus knotted with sporangiophores. Horsetail rush, or winter scouring rush because once used to clean pots, grows happily in shallow water. Its rigid stems laced with sand, all the better for scrubbing. Quiet in the diffuse light of my room, I listen to the pond outside, water splashing into itself among native iris, pickerel and zebra rush. Reflections waver over the panes of the window, water-marking the page. In the late evenings, gulf coast toads call from pond to plumeria, *come see, come see, come see.*

How know to know any place comes first to me through trees and birds, native plants. In *Florula Ludoviciana, A Flora of Louisiana*, I find a companion creature, often as uncertain as I am. First collected and recorded by C. S. Rafinesque then "Translated, Revised, and Improved, from the French of C. C. Robin" its plant names are often in error. Tracking them through the aegis of Google, most modern names come clear. Though in the end, I choose not to include their names with the images. Instead the entries become a reservoir from which I draw fragmented narratives. What might such language say of south Louisiana in 1817 translated by this means to the present? "cirriform/ like a star/ a real white/ and four." Of honeyvine, "some faint/ fruit and habit/ a stranger/ natural order." The exquisite common world everywhere feeds me. Which bird? Which vine? What sort of tree, whose thorned trunk thrusts sharp hooks from smooth, gray skin? Pressed flowers at the base of the page.

Through woods and trails, along canoe trails circumnavigating lakes, tramping into the woods, the ground alternately wet and dry, the quotidian chance of wet feet. The understory is thick with dwarf palmettos sending their broad fronds splay-like into the air or collapsed onto the ground: almost any vine makes the palmettos habitat, banana spiders spinning nets of golden silk between one frond and the next. South Louisiana names them after their long, curved orange- and amber-mottled abdomens. They are lovely spiders, happy stringing their traps in my garden between roses and roofline, or among the ragged woods of oak and pecan trees, of blackberry brambles where the horse and I pass, almost blithely though I keep a long stick handy for clearing the biggest ones. The horse flicks his tail at flies, and canters, left foreleg reaching out, white hind bright in the dust: a leafy desire roused by riding through these woods, finding balance as the horse accelerates across last spring's acorns and over a low fence. A white blaze and one white stocking for luck. When I brush him down after the ride, squirrels scold overhead and he nickers at his neighbors stamping in a line beside the weathered red of the barn. Behind the woods, wind soughs through a cane field, the sugar already eight feet high. Of banana spiders, the females eat the males after mating, a high protein meal before egg-laying, assuring the success of her clutch. At home, half-finished in pond-light, drawings wait on my return.

Réponds: What do you remember about the earth?

processes
plains :: mountains :: seas
      canyon   cañon

inverting the heights
accretion precipitation erosion

        stonetomud

       stone to mud

      st o ne to mu d

     s t o n e   t o   m u d

s t o n e t o m u d

neither/not ::

      stone

            sand

                loam

late pleistocene sediment

    lagoonal clay

     deltaic clay

    Mississippi alluvial loess

not dry
    ils naviguèrent les marécages en pirogue
    les bayous || swamp   wetland   bay

And the environment they came from. The trawlin,' the crabbin,' the shrimpin,' the trappin.' You know, the survival thing to do to make a living and survive. Well, when they'd get to the oilfield they'd use the same practical applications, you know? Let's try this see if it works. Let's try this. We used to do this. I remember when we did this with the boat. You know? We had to get it up we didn't have no...dry dock and we'd utilize this. You know? Just from life experience. They... applied that. When they went on their...on their jobs. And it didn't take them long to learn. And then....all the boat skippers were local people. From down the Bayou. Been on boats all their life. And they didn't need compasses. They didn't need...well they didn't have. They didn't even have compasses. Much less radar. But they didn't need compasses.

—Werlien Prosperie, July 9, 2003. Houma, LA.
Cajun musician and oilfield worker

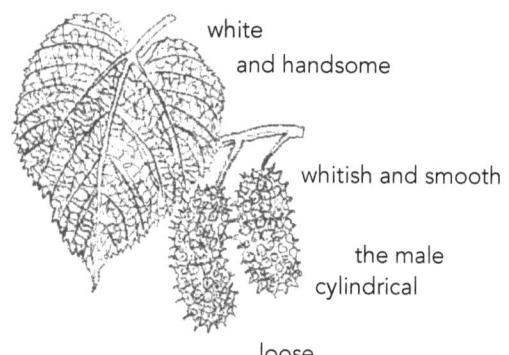

white
and handsome

whitish and smooth

the male
cylindrical

loose

Réponds: What this means

      snak

          -ing

(figure and

          ground)

             a means through

     nothing

certain

                  (((buoyed, bodied)

      watersupposing ground

what Texaco used: Jimmi Martin

on the bayou and
off the land
Texaco
Texaco

a sixty-five foot
a seventy-two foot boat
in the fisheries
in the fisheries

the oilfield
booming
a matter of
knowing

oil rigs
wooden rigs
Leeville and
Golden Meadow

pipelines in the marsh
hauling pipe
laying pipe in the marsh
like a

pie
in the sky
steady paycheck, and
fishing oysters

the small luggers
small wooden luggers
the oil companies
dumped

everything overboard
could fill
the Gulf up

the bay, or the lakes

fill the Gulf up with
can't hardly trawl
or we

dodging, these
long hangs
no regulation
regulation

trash
left on the bottom
cars, grating
file cabinets

desks, a sink
anything
went over the side
don't care what

over the side
ten foot deep

"We are all okay. It hit bad. We had plenty of trouble keeping things together with nothing much to do. Tannie and I took Olga and her two children, Glenn and Old Nora and her five children to high land until the storm was over. Now I am on the boat with Dada and Tannie, going back home…. We still did not have high gulf water but wind and sand blowing…I can't say if we will have a big loss. Some families will lose plenty."

—Zoe Cessac Sagrera, Chenier au Tigre,
September 20, 1943, *Louisiana Paradise*

Louisiana Toxics Release Inventory (TRI)

The EPA tracks the management of certain toxic chemicals that may pose a

thereupon

threat to human health and the environment. Total onsite and off-site disposal or other releases: 140.4 million lbs from 389 companies. Most prevalent toxics released: Acetonitrile, Ammonia, Methyl, Methacrylate, Cyanide compounds. Louisiana ranks 5 out of 56 states/ territories nationwide based on total releases per square mile

(Rank 1 = highest releases), 2015.

(https://iaspub.epa.gov/triexplorer/tri_factsheet.factsheet_forstate?&pstate=LA&pyear=2015&pParent=TRI&pDataSet=TRIQ1)

...Grand Terre is going: the sea mines her fort, and will before many years carry the ramparts by storm. Grand Isle is going, —slowly but surely; the Gulf has eaten three miles into her meadowed land. Last Isle has gone!
—Lafcadio Hearn, *Chita*

seven feet

branched like a pea

sweet

to clean and scour

Lapse :: a city

       the city shifts on its piers   :: a local vernacular

                                         inundation   subsidence

down-warping alluvial earth   flood control and

            navigational   concerns chat like

    laughing gulls on

                   levees   lithosphere

                merely mud

    river's ancient deposition bird-

foot   shallow   sea

the weight of things   :: highways   bridges   rectilinear city

        sprawling toward   water

              coteau :: maiden cane   and arrowhead

things of the past

                    sea   rising over

                            narrow shoals

                                          hydrology

                            of channelization

          sun king's   flooded realm   le Conseil

     Souverain   erodes

                            a brackish hem ::

        salt grass and   wire grass

                    lapse toward

      fresh canouche

              city wrapped within

                            by the river rapt

Plaquemine Aquifer

> *"It was a beautiful spring morning—warm & quiet with mists."*
> —Dorothy Wordsworth

it was a beautiful contaminant transport
a beautiful original source area
beautiful probable source

& quiet solid phases eroded
quiet turbulent river flow
quiet cut-bank

it was a beautiful turn in the stream
a beautiful channel each
beautiful shift to the outside turn

& quiet any contaminant
quiet any released at or
quiet near site 13

it was a beautiful fluvial process
a beautiful site 13
beautiful facilitated the movement

& quiet cutting tends to be
quiet prominent at the likely
quiet significant source

it was a beautiful direct ((in direct)) contact
a beautiful upper sand aquifer
beautiful once contaminants moved

& quiet Plaquemine Aquifer
quiet aquifer
quiet upper sand

it was a beautiful transport
a beautiful Mississippi River transport
beautiful dispersed away

& quiet processes ((advection and
quiet dispersion)) contribute to
quiet plume growth

it was a beautiful lateral stream
cutting a beautiful pipeline
beautiful accelerated descent

& quiet cutting there
quiet vinyl chloride
quiet cis-1,2dichlorethene

it was a beautiful 1 foot per day
a beautiful rough estimate
beautiful spreading

& quiet indicated by
quiet purpose
quiet an idea of

it was a beautiful order of magnitude
a beautiful contaminant reach
beautiful Myrtle Grove wells

& quiet 20-40 year
quiet time frame
quiet 1964 Dow dioxin

it was a beautiful [formerly Morrisonville] spill
a beautiful racial
beautiful profiling of chemical

& quiet plant placement
quiet likely significant source
quiet area in black

it was a beautiful ((color line
a beautiful color line)) does not rule out
beautiful does not

& quiet rule out
quiet 1993 release
quiet the contaminated material

it was a beautiful no longer identifiable on the surface
a beautiful vinyl-
beautiful chloride in ground water

& quiet 97ppb
quiet drinking water
quiet Myrtle Grove water supply

        only the calyx
    admitting

      doubtful

                its natural

              affinity

                  might also be
akin

Réponds: What this means (2)

> what this means
>   what any

                          distance
                          answers

    what matters

> meaning this also
>   asking
>   *what*   waters
>
> what you're asking

      ((peri-tactical
    meaning

>   any such
>   any such waters

matter
no matter

                    water

              water ll (para)tactical
                (-taxa a matter of

> what water gathers
>
> what   this
>
>   gather

                asks

watering the ground

current of geography

1
adrift on a current of geography
here ‖ now
a movement like breath
scaffolding time:

    insect hum   bird call   water spill
         leaf rattle
    oak pollen & oak catkins drift in the air collect
    on every surface vernal
    shower of oaks south
    Louisiana douses itself in male gametes turns
    chartreuse while azaleas beckon white
    and blushed wanton
    seed making

2
time (re)asserts itself generationally
if I stop
moving do I occupy the same
place or has
history left me behind

    larks still call from lemon trees dart
    in low trajectory from
    lemon to oak
    shallow goblets of rose scent wave
    on pressure of wind, this
    breeze traversing another (felt) space

3
walking as rest
here   now   there
gather laundry before rain
or wash
my hair
read voraciously
outdoors
ignoring the summons to
day and duty:
small carp carve algae with orange mouths
green giving way to black water
spills into itself
a long trough introducing sound and
oxygen lemon
blossom brushes its scent over my skin
and spring stays
here   where I stop

Myrtle Grove Trailer Park

rows of sugar cane
hard against

                                               "we all had miscarriages"

dented but decent
smothered steak and stewed
PLAK-uh-mun trailers

a community ceases to
exist   what was not
said   a word

not— Louisiana
Hospitals and
Human Services

a word—
failed to, failed
vinyl

-chloride in the water
report
to report Myrtle Grove

                                               "And I thought—"

Dow Chemical
working to pin-
point the source

((part of the   *"I hope—"*
solution ((source)) the plant
is <u>not</u> the source   *"—I don't lose my baby"*

5 years
"human error"
failure to report to tell

vinyl-
chloride
detected in Upper Plaquemine Aquifer

jobs for more than
6000 Dow and
contract employees

part of the surrounding
community balancing
economic environmental and

:: big shade trees
trailers with porches
social responsibility

splash pools men
washing cars   "we all just went—"
empty space brown

patches people and
homes
gone wind

blows in off the cane   "—on with life, cooking with it"
Dow's "pure product"
((1964 PVC

production))
no knowing how 5 years
Dow "working

to be part of the solution"
toxic
grounds already condemned

Morrisonville ((cemetery))   "Thirteen—"
contaminated water   miscarrying
                                          "—That many women on one street?"

Dow in Louisiana
children throng from
the school bus afternoon

cools
re-
locating on checks al-

ready spoken for
    (("part of the solution"))
                                          "a nice place"

Réponds: Whom do you love?

kin

woods

roses

sweet ll canouche

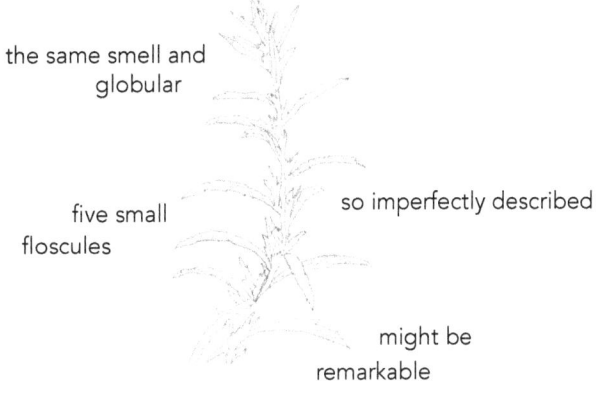

the same smell and
globular

five small
floscules

so imperfectly described

might be
remarkable

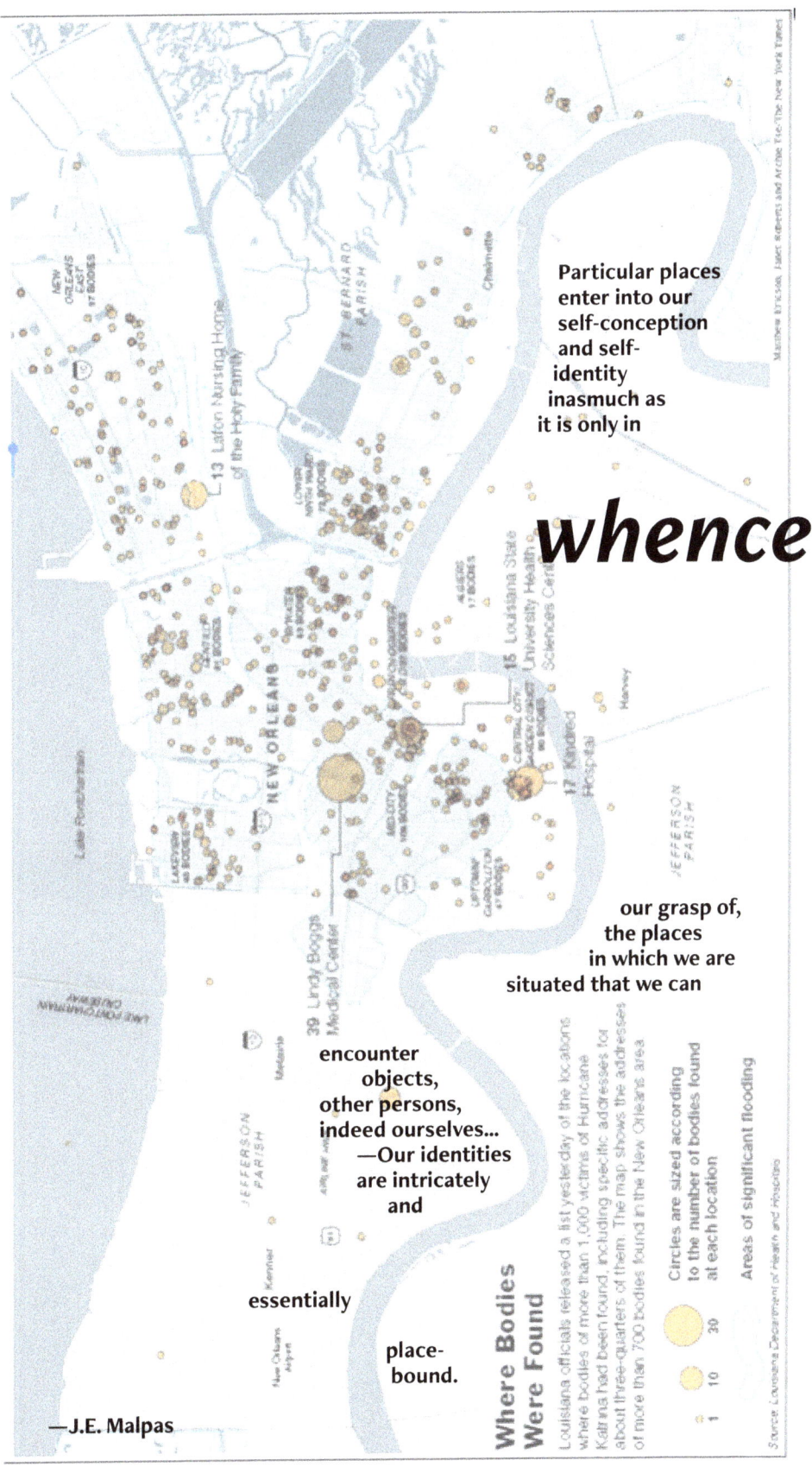

Particular places enter into our self-conception and self-identity inasmuch as it is only in

whence

our grasp of, the places in which we are situated that we can encounter objects, other persons, indeed ourselves... —Our identities are intricately and essentially place-bound.

—J.E. Malpas

Where Bodies Were Found

Louisiana officials released a list yesterday of the locations where bodies of more than 1,000 victims of Hurricane Katrina had been found, including specific addresses for about three-quarters of them. The map shows the addresses of more than 700 bodies found in the New Orleans area.

"I want to assure the people of the affected areas and this country that we'll deploy the assets necessary to get the situation under control....we'll get on top of this situation. and we're gonna help people that need help."
　　　　　　　　—President George Bush, Sept 3, 2005

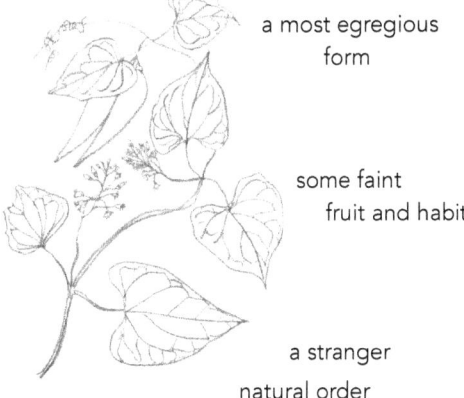

a most egregious
form

some faint
fruit and habit

a stranger
natural order

KATRINA

HURRICANE KATRINA...A MOST DEVASTING HURRICANE WITH UNPRECENDENTED STRENGTH...RIVALLING THE INTENSITY OF HURRICANE CAMILLE IN 1969. MOST OF THE AREA WILL BE UNIHABITABLE FOR WEEKS...PERHAPS LONGER. AT LEAST ONE HALF OF WELL-CONSTRUCTED HOMES WILL HAVE ROOF AND WALL FAILURE. ALL GABLED ROOFS WILL FAIL.
—National Hurricane Center, Saturday, August 28, 10:11am

Les haricots sont pas salés...

Saturday, August 28

At 10am, Mayor Nagin issues the first ever mandatory evacuation order for city of New Orleans: *"I want to emphasize, the first choice of every citizen should be to leave the city."*

some strengthening   some   27 miles of marsh
  ((disappeared))   stormsurge
forecast   and coastal
near impossible to focus   erosion

roof and   a toxic
not   "if"   failure

built on a sponge   residential low ground
stagnation grounding   stability
dumping ground   "hazmat
no   guidance or   gumbo"

sufficient   31 super-
        fund sites   we may call
pending further   for a *voluntary*
        had no   was no
list of   evacuation priorities

people with   *a priori*
    special needs   and 112,000 without
    cars without   "the mayor was-
    no 72-hour window   remaining
-nervous"   marketed as
    candor

Brownie   waiting to see   no

        buses coming   for them for for
special   needs   for
-gotten

                                  for
                                  -saken   Bush va-

cationing at the ranch   needing what (?)
out in the wet   old and   left
     needy   behind

                        people

    took   *pride*   *owning those*   *little*
Ninth Ward   *shacks*[11]

---

[11] Oliver Thomas, City Councilman representing the Ninth Ward

Saturday, August 28

"The combination of Katrina winds and no electricity led to a night full of bright stars. Just gorgeous, you know, it made you feel all right. Or so, for few fleeting minutes, we pretended."
—James O. Byrne, *Times-Picayune* writer

8am (918 mb Superdome "shelter of last
Advisory 23::   maximum sustained winds increased to
resort" 175 mph Category 5

hurricane 5 inches of water
down South White Street a river

flood walls top ping 600 911
calls mostly New Orleans East
Lakeview Ninth Ward "I can't
get out of my attic. The water is

up to my—"

Lakeview marshy
spillover area flash flood near   Ninth
    Ward inundated by Mirabeau Bridge
attic or canoe? washout only

2nd stories above water
    an odd

glow roads now glood aglow

no police communication and water like

geysers out of sewers
the need for repairs Congress' habitual
diversion of funding from floos
protection projects an
engineering flaw
something
something shifted
17th Street Canal
no FEMA
2000

shelter
    in the Super Dome more ((already)) standing in line

Monday, August 30: Devastation Tour

```
Fox                                  News in the Quarter
high and                      dry "a pregnant lady with
a shopping cart cop                           baby supplies and a
"Stop, lady!"                 stop

people wading through             debris commandeering supplies
"people are                   dying here
"so poor and so               black"
people                        desperate and the cops
        don't                 to prioritize rescue
give-a-shit                   and compassion "How do you

prepare for this?"¹²          Where the     500
FEMA buses                         inching toward marshal law
400 Nat'l Guard troops        marooned           by the Industrial Canal
        breach    Nagin            terrified
for his own    safety

                              Lake Bourgne

                bursts                            down MRGO¹³ an
        800 foot                    breach    8:14am
   ::hiding out at                                    the Hyatt

     9am Ninth Ward in 6          feet
of water                 St. Bernard in deep and     rising
quickly St. Rita's             unevacuated   20 minutes
        nursing home                flooded to the ceiling
   Chalmette                              14 feet in 10 minutes "I just

                assumed I was dead"¹⁴          FEMA's single
agent in New Orleans sends          urgent emails to Brown
        food    water   medical aid    the city
              80% of the city    under water former

head of horseshowjudging          Brownie    "out   of his depth"
"I don't know                           where that information went."¹⁵
```

---

¹² Commander Tim Ballard, Vice and Narcotics NOPD
¹³ Mississippi River-Gulf Outlet
¹⁴ Nita Hutter, St. Bernard Parish State Representative re: detailed request for FEMA aid
¹⁵ Marty Bahamonde, New Orleans' only FEMA official as Katrina approached

Monday, August 30 :: nightfall

"People were happy to see reporters. They knew that somebody would tell their story. They were right. We did. But they also believed that people would rush to their assistance. This was America, after all. Boy, were they wrong in that regard!"
—James O. Byrne, *Times-Picayune* writer

not one to   offer to
"write a blank check" Bush
         financial   looking into the
federal response   obligations of the
                                   ((   ))

                                        temperatures in the Dome
90 degrees plus   fetid   humid
food and water almost   gone the
Natl Guard   "edgy"   no choice but to
 lock the doors

                          survivors flood

         west to   Convention Center

                      Morial   more dead than   alive
     no   weapon searches   no Guardsmen
     no   press   shit

         everywhere   in the   Auguste 29
before the hurricane   hit
         Homeland Security   predicts both levee
              breaching and floods   leaving "the Metro Area

         submerged for weeks   or months"
                 Good Morning   America   President
Bush avers   "I don't think...

              I don't think anyone

                                    I don't think anyone

              anticipated   anticipated the
                      breach of levees."

Tuesday, August 31

> "We winged it."
> —Lt. Commander Jimmy Duckworth, U.S. Coast Guard

    diy rescues   Lakeview
                                        Ninth Ward
                                        Seventh Ward
                                        St. Bernard Parish
    ski-doos canoes flat-bottomed boats

NOLA Homeboys
Dyan "Mama D" French Cole and the Soul Patrol
LA Fish and Wildlife
Mitch Landrieu

      one rule   "Paddle around
                                   "save people
                                   "survive"

1 7 t h   S t r e e t   C a n a l   b r e a c h   w i d e n e d   t o   5 0 0   f e e t

                                      47 rescue copters
finally in the sky   Coast   Guard
Operation   Dunkirk
            1,200 rescued by   nightfall

    folk
           stranded in the city   overpasses
                                     Superdome
                                     Convention Center
                                   streets attics   rooftops
                                                         corpses
                                                                  everywhere

offers of help   aircraft rubber boats dump trucks vans trained personnel
    law enforcement pour   in to FEMA

FEMA: "Request   denied"

                                       mid-day Chertoff
           "really caught...by surprise"

                    ((news of the levee break

reached the administration   Monday, 7:30am)) Cheney Montana fly-fishing
President Bush   in guitar
                                                  photo-op

I saw 5,000 African Americans on the I-10 Causeway desperate, perishing, dehydrated, babies dying….Africans in the hull of a slave ship.[16]

---

[16] Rev. Jesse Jackson speaking to CNN's Anderson Cooper.

Tuesday, August 31: raw crude

Murphy Oil, down low, keeping an eye, the down low, on costs set up, set up shop in St Bernard Parish. Refining oil. On low-lying land. Refinery in the lea of MRGO's storm surge excess. Excess (profit) siphoned off. Gambled and. Lost. Tank 250-2, lost. Not full, not empty. Not filled with water as a precaution, and. Floated away. Adrift. In the flood, west through streets and houses of Meraux and Chalmette. Floated

1.1 million gallons of crude. Floated, 1700 modest homes "never going to get that clean."[17] Parks, schools, sidewalks, roads. Birds, nutria, small animals, abandoned dogs. Oil. Mired in oil. Trapped in. Mired, fumes and. Muck. Stuck. No contamination gear, no ventilation. Floated

raw crude's benzo(a)pyrene, diesel and oil range organic chemicals, arsenic. Exceed. Exceeds screening levels. In the air. On water. In the soil, U.S. EPA: "Children and pets should not enter the oil contaminated area." Protect skin, open windows and doors, wear boot covers so as not to track oil about. Skin burns, rashes, central nervous system damage, depression, convulsions.

[16] Murphy Oil employee Shepard Brown to *USA Today*.

Wednesday, September 1[18]

"Guys, this is bigger than what we can handle. This is bigger than what FEMA can do. I am asking for help."
    —Michael Chertoff call to the White House, Tuesday night.

skimming under   traffic lights   street lamps
boats move house to house   tunnel hulls   aluminum vessels   bay boats
   homemade johnboats
         X

volunteer   Lake Arthur Lake Charles Cajun Navy
   people stranded in   the sun   on overpass in wheelchairs

 "begging us for water"   'looters' supply   food and water   elderly and

marooned
      bodies   on fences
         railroad tracks

   Reverend Willie Walker   borrows a Red
          Cross t-shirt
            gets past

         the cops
    pulling people from the flood

NOLA homeboys

     plucking   folk from the bilge   where
    FEMA?   Red   Cross?
     "the DOT doesn't
       do ambulances"[19]

  cops trash talk   the left-
behind
    "fire ants"   "dumb
       niggers"

  Charmaine Neville   in a Canal Street city bus
          ((commandeered

her neighbors   a full busload
   X   out of the bowl
    free to   Shekinah Full

---

[18] pray-painted red X's used to indicate a flooded home has been searched.
[19] Robert Block, *Wall Street Journal*, September 13, 2005

           Glory Baptist Church
                                      George Bush still
                    riding it out in   Texas   Brownie "any-
                thing we need to do
                                              or tweak?"
getting a meal in BR
                       between emails

          and Karl Rove   roving through
                         keeps   Gov. Blanco from getting
                              help turn
                                       a blue state red?

          American Bus Association can't
get through   to FEMA   ((FEMA))
                                  contracted
                 Landstar trucking (no   buses) no buses
                                                political
       friendships   ((Chamber of   Commerce))
$400 million
                                 buses coming
                                                    X
             5 days   late

                              a PR   blitz
                                              churning out
       blame   Blanco's
                  fault   "The White House is saying…"
                                                        not Bush's not
                Bush's fault though
Schwarzenegger sends
                     8 Swift Water Rescue Teams
            500   Natl Guard   medical personnel
                     boats food radios water

         at the Dome just   enough
MREs   one per
                  and water
                         LA Natl Guard
              triaging   X

:: This is not the time to play the   WHITE HOUSE update
                                              blame game ::

  flying over   -head Air Force   One taking in
                                                    the view

Thursday, September 2

> "This is a national disgrace. FEMA has been here three days, yet there is no command and control. We can send massive amounts of aid to tsunami victims but we can't bail out the city of New Orleans?"
> —Terry Ebberts, New Orleans Homeland Security

                                                                                        weak and   confused (?)

                awol (?)   bereft   (   )   and bigger
fish to fry taking the   fight to the terrorists

                    children   separated from   parents
stranger   s in their own—

                                                     refugees
                                        walking I-10 to Baton Rouge

> *black*
>
> *poor*
>
> *from Louisiana*

buses arrive   four or   five at a time

                                       folk wait   on causeways
            "This is…"

                            Louisiana   stifling heat
                  "..tough to witness"[20]
                                             X

US Route 90   >   Gretna   little damaged
   6000 evacuees crossing the
                                           Crescent City Connection
           cops fire   shots
              "necessary   force"
             over their heads
        "Get the fuck off the bridge" "
                         ….keep those
  X   fucks out of here"

---

[20] Brian G. Lukas, WWL-TV cameraman

15,000 inside the   convention center
5000   outside
                    hospitals hiring
                         medivacs Charity and University
         can't   pay   can't—

                              Hollygrove under
                    8 feet of water while white   X
                                   businesses high and

General Honoré "This is not…"

> Where is the help?
> Where are the buses?

   "…Iraq."   No   buses for the convention

                                             center Mr.
Chertoff "I   have not heard of thousands…"

> We don't have food. We don't have water.   X
>
> Are you really going to make us sit here like this?

         "…of people at the convention center
                         who don't have food and water."

Friday, September 3: "not going exactly right"[21]

> "The contact is the dimension—as literally as you would like to understand that word in which communication takes place."
> —Timothy Morton, *Ecology Without Nature*

"Check, check, check." Superdome nearly emptied. No records of these. X "Can you hear me?" Transports. Who went, who where. "Check one,…" No records. "…two." 5,068 children missing. 12,514 adults. "Do you copy?" Reported. Nearly. 2000-3000 left. Space a body takes up. Or air. "Over." 700 Hyatt guests and workers put to the head of the line. "Copy."

President Bush meets Gov. Blanco and Mayor Nagin at Louis Armstrong Airport

The contact dimension, airline highway. Evacuees bloody, exhausted. "Break- X break. Copy?" X Dehydrated, on foot, pushing wheelchairs. Down airline highway. Communicating distress. "Do you copy?" Converge at roadblock. "Am I coming through?" A Presidential lock-, on lockdown. Feet swollen, a cart, two babies wrapped in plastic, dead.

"Given the dire circumstances…things are going relatively well."[22]

"Come in." "Check, check." Locked down, airport lockdown. "Do you-?" Perished. President Bush 'coptering. In. "Mayday…" From the 17th Street Canal. "…mayday." "There's a lot of crying…people in pain. An elderly woman has just been brought into the morgue."[23]

X Ill and injured come in by helicopter, ambulance. Triage

The phatic dimension. Radio signals, vibrating air molecules. Bush dead. Set on "federalizing" National Guard in Louisiana. Emphatic. "Do you copy?" *Phatikos*: affirming. Though not in Haley Barbour's Mississippi. "Can you hear me? Over."

A quick in and out

---

[21] President Bush speaking in Alabama on his first visit to the Gulf since Katrina.
[22] Michael Chertoff, Secretary of Homeland Security, 2005-2009
[23] Brian G. Lukas, WWL-TV

Saturday, September 4

"There was a period of days when we weren't sure who was directing the federal response and were all the actions being taken."
    —Richard Falkenrath, Homeland Security Advisor, 2001-2004

1:05 am EST President   Bush signs
    deployment orders
        U.S. Army 82nd Airborne   Division

X
25,000   angry and exhausted
  people still at   Morial Convention Center
    dispatchers: 1,000   emergency rescue calls

9am-6pm buses finally clear   the convention center

                  Spreading the blame
                        quick and
                            thick
                    X
"As of Saturday, Blanco still had not declared
a state of emergency, the senior Bush official said."[24]

house-
    to-house searches

              X   a city under

                          water
the 82nd "instantly
    stabilized
      command and control"[25] six days into the flood

X   FEMA finalizes bus request
                    "government planners did not
  X   predict such a disaster ever could

---

[24] Washington Post, 9/4/05. Correction issued hours later. Gov. Blanco had declared a state of emergency Friday, th th August 26 , and forwarded the letter to the White House Saturday August 27 , requesting the President declare a federal state of emergency for Louisiana.

[25] Terry Ebbert, New Orleans Office of Homeland Security

Superdome clear   5pm
           five feet

                deep in trash   X
                                    X
                                            X
    Houston
           hospitality   250, 000 evacuees
                       X
           grateful dry fed   bereft

      X
     X   X

                        "so many of the people in the arena here, you
                             know, were underprivileged anyway,
                                              so this,
                                           this is working
                                        very well for them."²⁶

         X

 X

                        X

---

²⁶ Former First Lady Barbara Bush, Monday, September 5, 2005 (American Public Media)

September 24

                        Hurricane

      Rita   ((sustained winds

                            120mph))

makes   landfall

                      between   Sabine Pass

    Texas and

                        Hollybeach

                  Louisiana

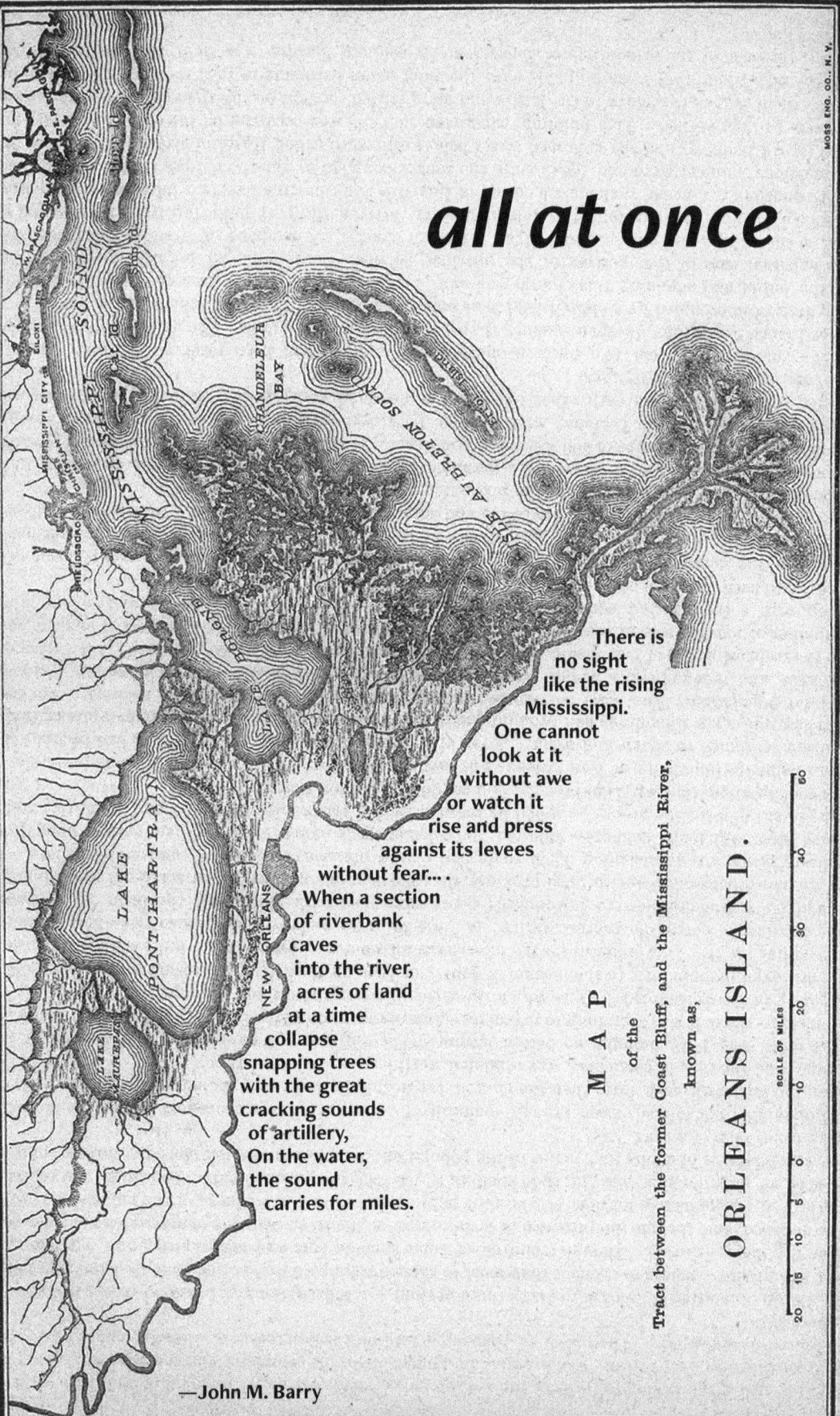

all at once

There is no sight like the rising Mississippi. One cannot look at it without awe or watch it rise and press against its levees without fear.... When a section of riverbank caves into the river, acres of land at a time collapse snapping trees with the great cracking sounds of artillery, On the water, the sound carries for miles.

—John M. Barry

Caspian tern: **(k)urh(t)** *u tut (squeeze throat tight) — vibrate the r sound — almost a click, then drawn out like a hoarse quack*

Laughing Gull: er-it, er-it, er-it, **ah!-ah!-ah!-ah!** *(like a laugh — through a squeezed throat, each "ah" sharply enunciated)*

Brown Pelican: **ert. ert. ert. ert.** *(the throat squeezed tight, each "ert" discrete) — like a seal, squeaky & bubbly*

the small lakes
white
shining
nearly winged

yellow

a fragrant
common

affinity

has some

Barataria Bay

Plaquemines Parish takes its name from the French translation of the word piakimin in the native Mobilean trade language. Persimmon country, oak country. We drive south from New Orleans following the course of the Mississippi to West Point La Hache, past orange groves, cattle grazing, past infamous Caernarvon [27]. Post-Katrina fishing camp houses loom above us on piers. Plaquemines Parish flows past, ordinary and strange, a human landscape of make-do in response to unrelenting wind, water, sinking land. Houses hover on pilings above the next flood. Levees, taming the sprawling impulse of the river to escape its banks and wander, inadvertently send land-building silt out over the continental shelf. Diversion projects pipe a slender fraction of the silty water into Barataria Bay, giving rise to patches of luxuriant sweetmarsh.

We stop for peaches along the way, before driving on to Woodland Plantation. Built by river captain William Johnson, Woodland was once a sugar plantation. Before building the "big house", however, Johnson kept enslaved Africans in four two-story brick buildings on site: a partnership with the pirate Jean Lafitte who abducted them from slave ships offshore, bringing the captives in secret up Grand Bayou. The enslaved Africans were then retailed up and down the river to labor on plantations. Woodland Plantation now houses tourists in the antebellum 'splendor' of its yellow galleries below the west bank of the river. Ultimately swept away by Hurricane Betsy, the slave quarters have been supplanted by flowering gardens, where bees, ants, and mosquitos liven the thick, damp heat of summer.

In the morning, settled in a fishing boat, we head toward West Pointe La Hache Diversion Project in Barataria Bay. The boat carries us through narrow channels in the marsh that quickly give way to wider channels, "cuts" made to accommodate oil exploration and drilling. The channels continually widen, their girth hauling saltwater inland out of the Gulf, killing sweetmarsh. As the marsh dies, the muddy earth washes away, taking with it the complex communities of plants, fish, birds, and other animals that therein throve.

The world is flat here. Water and marsh grass spread out to the horizon in every direction. Less than twenty minutes into the marsh, we are surprised by a pair of dolphins near the boat. Hunting fish along the skirts of the marsh, they have followed the fish up the salt highway through black rush and oyster grass. Though astonishing, the dolphins are a sign of how endangered these wetlands have become.

Our guide turns the boat, follows another channel: green and yellow marsh extending away from us wherever we look. This channel, though narrower, is still wide. He tells us how many is no sign of trees, except the skeletons of salt-killed

---

[27] At the behest of New Orleans civic leaders, the levees on the westward loop in the river at Caernarvon were blasted open making a shortcut to the sea. The channel released 250,000 cubic feet of water per second, destroying the homes and property of 10,000 displaced people. Families were compensated for pennies on the dollar. The effort ultimately was unnecessary, as a natural break in the new Orleans levee relieved the pressure anyway.

oaks, cheniers the only high ground out in the wet. Our guide takes us down Grand Bayou, past the remnant community, fifty souls, more or less, who still make their living shrimping and oystering. Most houses huddle in some progression of collapse, damaged by Hurricane Katrina. Seeking the protection of land further inland, nearly all the community left after the storm's destruction, its surge marching easily through the wide passes cut through the marsh. Our guide tells us that only two or three generations past, people could still reach the community by road. Now the children travel to school by yellow school boat.

As our craft glides closer to the diversion project, the marsh gradually changes, expanses of cut up wetland giving way to increasingly bird-filled, diverse wetlands, lush where the heavily vegetated banks sprawl over the water and the water loses clarity, red and muddy with river silt. Only four of the eight pipes run most days, according to our guide. Still, an extraordinary difference in this narrow patch where the river water's silt reaches. Redwing blackbirds, herons, egrets, flycatchers. Wildflowers along the banks, turtles in the water.

We return the way came, silent, the trembling prairie quickly becoming more water than earth. Complexity gives way to salt marsh, flycatchers to seagulls roosting on the piers of Grand Bayou. In 2012 Plaquemines Parish became the highest oil producing parish in the state, pulling over 14 million barrels from of the fragile marshes of the coas

Water and history (2): Macondo Prospect

> *"[the impact of oil spill in the Gulf will be] very, very modest"*
> —Tony Hayward, BP CEO

beneath the surface
1500 feet
what does not weather

                        layers of warm and cool water
                        ::smooth cordgrass
                        ::black needle rush
                        collide

April 20, 9:45 pm, 5
minutes to

                        osprey
                        egret
                        alligator

escape failed
deadman's switch 11
‖ dead ‖

                        roseate spoonbill barrier
                                island *les isles dernières*
                        Raccoon ‖ Whiskey ‖ Trinity ‖ East ‖
                        Wine

deep
        circulation

                        :: beaver in wild millet
                        dowitchers lesser
                        yellow leg

"it is not possible to
assure its success"
or any—

                        sea purslane
                        salt
                                  heliotrope
                        deltaic mudflat   sprawl

illusion
a hundred
thousand others

                        its seedy tangle
                        mat-like
                        black
                        tar-oiled surf

there is no
cost to us or the environment

                                conspicuous
                                              saline marsh

(parenthetically   speaking

                                azure tropic   oiled
                                seabirds oiled
                                fish dolphin

subsea dispersants
oil llfailed   failed
domes switches pipe-
lines   faith

                                intertidal   perennial
                                salt grass sea
                                shallow
                                          blue water

trapped below the surface
one million dollars a day
running behind

                                —basin, deep
                                water coral garden
                                coastal
                                                        rookeries
                                /grass given to sea

dead man's   dead
rush behind
schedule failed
              blow-out

                                a shrub-like
                                herb with yellow flowers

preventer keeping oil
cheap and available

                                passerine songbirds needle rush
                                edging the marsh

                                or memory

this apparatus "re-
mains a new technology"

                                    avender wolfberry blossoms
                                    margin the marsh
                                    sea cane long
                                                    grass

5000 feet below the surface we
"remain uncertain" hedging
our bets doubts there are no
(assurances) or

                                    goldenrod's small
                                    yellow flowers

need for undue
concern
alarm, though brackish

                                    to four feet (willowy
                                    salt grass
                                    glasswort
                                                    dodder

strangle-vine, strangle-
hold BP will
do all in its power to
(maximize profits) pay all
legitimate claims
(minimizing losses /
culpability—

            5000 feet below the surface who
            could have known
            knew this
            hive
            of nurseries   bluefin
                Kemp's Ridley sea turtles

                                    oysters   shrimp   brown
                                            pelicans blue

                        crab

gulf "BP will continue
to promptly provide all
information necessary"

not   at all
necessary
quantifying "the incident"
is difficult
or assigning blame

                                      shrimpers oysterers fishers
                                      Bayou Fourchon boats idling
                                      setting   boom
                                      cleaning   :: dunlits
oil spill oil— "a
single distinct event"
minor   *casual*   *subordinate*, no

                                      willets   plovers
                                      oil from the beach—

catastrophe
methane gas rising rapidly into the column bursting
seals barriers Halliburton's nitrogen
foamed cement/non-
functional pod/BOP/decision-making apparatus we—
remains unsealed
standard
operating procedure
                               brown pelicans
                               yellow-eyed
                                            egrets

                               blue herons
                               night herons
                               wading birds
                                          along Gulf's
                               edge

accidental
injury shredded
annular failed
pressure tests over-
ridden BP six
weeks over schedule (drilling
                             Plaquemines Parish
                   piakimin   persimmon
                        waterandland *place*

targets) fed into the rig's generators
methane forced
upward under
pressure of oil released at the site of entry
who

knew/know
no
accurate measure
pressure test
certainty: mud-concrete-mud
seawater
sea—

                                                             buoyant and
                                                             labile gulf sea
                                                             loop
                                                                         current
                                                             oil
                                                             corexit
                                                                         dispersant

                    cloud
                    mat
                    plume

                    reach

                                                                     "celebrating the project's safety record"—

                    "a sudden catastrophic failure of cement, the casing or both"

before exploding
720 million in clean-up
and compensation to-date

7 billion in profits first
3 months 2010

reel

"I want my life back."
—Tony Hayward, BP Oil CEO, 2010

a lace fretwork a mesh ‖ mapped over made ‖ (over) a gap ‖ inviting full out and down flowing ‖ Mississippi outfall disposal waste ‖ *go down* ‖ central plains down *there* (here) Rocky Mountains wear ‖ worn ‖ down where earthmade where mud ‖ clay clinging black mud clay ‖ mud feet and mud sea clumping black mud delta sea ‖ crude ‖ beach oysters redfish shrimp oiled ‖ sand black ‖ oil land ‖ black mud and black sand (this) night a near ‖ or (not) a Macondo ‖ miss (miss) you ‖ not any where *here* ‖ any moment naught thou ‖ shalt not shall ‖ drill shell dark shell ‖ dreams ‖ oysters shrimp drill down no ‖ frills deep oil dark down ‖ ooze wound ‖ worn ‖ down ‖ carve or cut curve away channeled trampled berth ‖ birthing ‖ pipe bed and pipelines lay pipe make a way make ‖ over ‖ midden done done-in ‖ coast ‖ quaking field (gold) field ‖ birdfoot gulf coast ‖ what (remains) ‖ reminds miss mist ‖ mist-rise over gold ‖ golden meadow (quaking) ‖ field missed (we) missed out ‖ moist lure sure our ‖ land our fishermen oystermen shrimpers oil men big big men big daddy daddy-oh ‖ hey daddy-man man-o-man we're ‖ we're no we're ‖ not there we're no ‖ where here ‖ nowhere not ‖ this coastless boast a bent toast but not ‖ no not here ‖ knotted here ‖ nope

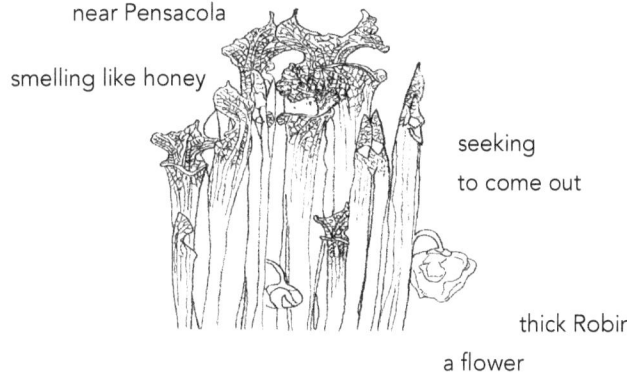

near Pensacola

smelling like honey

seeking
to come out

thick Robin
a flower

ALL AT ONCE | /// ||| ///

Réponds: What is the shape of your body? (2)

       bisected   pent
         water heading north

             erosion's r e a c h
      ((transect transact))

           bodyonloan

  water moves

                    an arrangement of

     tides   siltation

            immersion
         ((drowned

a sub
   -terranean zone of

       deferral   a done
  deal

         later, some
  time later

           might be
    parallax || paralysis

     dérangement

                 more or less wet

Lake Martin

In March, the rookery is alive with birds nesting. Great blue herons, roseate spoonbills, snowy egrets, great egrets, cattle egrets. A constant murmur of their talk fills the air. A barred owl drowses, nearly unseen, in the branches of a hickory tree. No sign of turtles or alligators: too cool this morning for sunning. In the low deciduous scrub at the edge of the cypress grove, little blue herons shelter apart from all the others. Dark slatey blue in color, their necks and head are deep maroon or purple. More brown than blue. Colonists like the other birds nesting at Lake Martin, invisible in their perch until the eye shifts focus, then little blues appear suddenly, in the middle range, dark with yellow eyes and greeny legs. Their chicks have white plumage with dusky tips, light and shadow among the leaves of the scrub. Midweek, no one else is here, the gravel road already dust.

Startled, a tangle of tiny alligators, five or six, tumble off a log into the shallow water. Only twelve to fifteen inches in length, stippled in yellow bands, their thick rough hides shine in the dappled glimmer. Their mother somewhere close by, unseen. Such sightings have been rare. Two nests carefully guarded, hatchlings swimming through reeds and rushes, a pair of little ones perched on their mother's back. More often, though still uncommon, adults sunning on the banks, owning all the world.

A month later, our kayaks skim easily over the lake surface, pushing through duckweed, clotted hyacinth. The lavender flower stalks of the hyacinth belie their wretched work: foreigners, like us, though better adapted to the heat. Deeper under the cypress and tupelo, a harder push through the lotus, last year's dry pods tipped on bent stems, a few seeds still cached within. End of April and already it is too hot. Or we are too late in the day to start. From the border where the cypresses end and open water begins, long-held duck blinds pose as tiny, brushy islands in the heart of the lake. Nothing moves, except herons, egrets, and spoonbills in their nests, shuffling, fanning their wings above the nests. Any breeze welcome. Last week, walking the back side of Lake Martin, we surprised ourselves by coming upon a sunning alligator sideways across the path. We left him to it, going back the way we came. Soon enough to get out of the sun anyway, into the shade of the trees. Cormorants cool off diving into the lake for sac-au-lait.

Water and history (3)

"...we thought the world was ours awright..."

channel trammel   water trending south
Bayou Fourchon
         more or less water
   moving there
marsh grass smooth cord grass common   reed

      "la vie fourchaise"
cheniers binding soaked
earth to earth old
shell heaps
    marais

boats   pole through *flottant*
drifting against
                                  blue

bull tongue   wire grass   islands

shrimpers oyster harvesters
"boat-minded people"
more or less
il est raide comme une babiche
amid the wet

profusion this
   trembling
          vegetative ground
luggers seining the flood

                          ::   ::

     Macondo

           blows out

                 h e m o r r h a g e s i n t o t h e G u l f

                   ::   ::

     shrimpers set
  nets

take   record hauls
turtle-by-catch excluders tied
shut the unlikely
            shapes of things

a regional syntax
    drifting

                before the slick

unoiled drowned
dead   tossed
back to sea

threnody

I keep the contents of my heart
stacked in wet clay
heavy with downpour
an all-consuming rut

the swamp has nothing
on moss and daub
or the shovel buried in my chest
mostly wet

and showed up late
a long cry from there
adjusting to the heat
shrivel and bloom

an abandoned churchyard
headdown in the rain
I think of plumeria, waxy and fragrant
horsetail woods

leaf-and-catkin wallow
against the rear door of the church
no matter
empathy only gets us so far

behind the grate small eyes
of an armadillo
its muted
reek of urine and feces

Water and history (4): Chandeleur Sound

A categorical exclusion, birdfoot deltaic lobe sprawling ‖ eastward. "No significant adverse impacts are expected"‖ a lapse, this piping plover brown pelican nursery ‖ Caspian and Sandwich terns diving against sludge ‖ catastrophe too "unlikely" no ‖ (additional) mitigation measures necessary, though urgency ‖obligatory (revenue management) abrogating safety and environmental— oil "plume" blanket, mantle ‖ smothering spongefields, corals, remnant cordgrass meadows ‖a lapse and rush, field of rushes fouled

Barrier islands braceletted in orange ‖royal terns, laughing gulls glide above (oiled) surf ‖pelicans given to loafing on shoals ‖ shelter dolphin sea turtles ‖ haven refuge home. This: investment portfolio, what's really at stake ‖ residual marsh toxicity, pompom booms mimicking widgeon-grass ‖ a regulatory regime cut-to-fit Big Oil, profit, thirst of our ‖ idealized machines ‖ fill in the blank ‖ "No clear strategic objectives"—tern estuary, soak, seat ‖ "linked to statutory requirements." What is required?

Profit, 93 million dollars a day ‖"No adverse", not ‖ part of the scheme ‖ copepods grazing on corexit, this ‖ web feeding squid, sperm whales, dolphin ‖ MMS like BP leashing science to production, acquisition ‖ *Yield* ‖ meaning to take, to harvest ‖ accumulate wealth at the bottom of things ‖ counting our blessings and breathing in fumes ‖ larval bluefin, swordfish this ‖ hydrocarbon nursery ‖ "adverse impacts" cannot ‖ be expected ‖ Or imagined ‖ preparing the bottom line ‖ thousands of frigate birds roosting amid black mangroves stabilizing the coast

No detailed environmental analysis ‖ necessary ‖ the exigencies of greed ‖ keeping us grounded ‖ coral reef widgeon-grass meadow another ‖ pipe dream ‖ illusion feeding on (corexit and oil suspension) dreams ‖ shrimp bed and oyster bed ‖ better this: cheap petrol, road going everywhere nowhere ‖ trading covenant, land, law, and our ‖ "good intentions" ‖ for jobs-in-the-industry ‖ *the industry* ‖ Selling ‖ out ‖ Down and— ‖ Kissing it goodbye, Chandeleur ‖ Sound, a categorical exclusion

Clean-up

A month after the blowout in the Gulf, a friend and I drive south along Bayou Lafourche: crab shacks and thrift shops, shrimp boats moored in the channel. We buy a bag of satsumas at the roadside, peel and eat them on our way. A.O. Rappelet Road (3090) takes us past Kajun Truck Plaza, Fourchon Beach RV Park, the sea plane base, Chevron Road. At Port Fourchon we pull off into a makeshift parking lot. Pickups and earthmoving equipment hunker over the Mini.

Beach cordoned off, a sheriff escorts us past men in rubber boots and gloves stuffing oiled sea wrack into bags. "The grandkids love it here. We always brought them for a swim and picnic." Fish plucked from the water for supper. A black tide line of crude-spoiled sand wanders beside us, as we walk toward the jetty at the west end of the beach. A clean-up crew scoops tar balls, oiled debris, soiled sand into bags wearing gloves, rubber boots, little else by way of protection. At the jetty, gazing across the horizon west to east, only in the middle range do leggy oil platforms disappear from view. Behind us, storage tanks, giant steel sheds, tugs, cranes, Cajun Iron Workers, Inc. Oilfield metropolis.

An ironic correspondence, Macondo Prospect takes its name from Gabriel Garcia Marquez's cursed town. I think of Jose Arcadio II, his blood inexplicably wending its way home to his father's house. Deepwater Horizon "over budget and behind schedule," the rig manager sent to "learn about deep water": we come to witness tragedy. *An ideal region of rural felicity.* Floating orange boom bellies up to the slick, oil hauled 5000 feet up to the surface. Bachelard claims, "Every force has a sex." I wonder about the force of 4.9 million barrels of oil hemorrhaging into the Gulf. Somehow BP CEO Tony Haywood manages to sleep: "The Gulf of Mexico is a very big ocean." Skimmer ships, floating boom, controlled fires. 1.84 million gallons of Corexit.

Later, back at the port, a contractor strikes up conversation, has some information he can't share here. "Call me later." What do we imagine he'll say? Alone among an army of men, he's looking for sex. Ideological assumptions underlie everything. Eleven men dead. Eleven.

Drill, baby. Drill.

gulf coast toad

rrreeeeeeeee(ehhh)
gulf coast toad
coastal plain toad   cloud blanket
persied - **rrruuh**
shower
waning   **uuuuuuhh**
rrreeeeeeeee(ehh) cloud
crescent
august   comet
black por-
ceiling   wigle
rrruuuh-uuuu(hh)
debris
green silk strands scatter
rrreeeeeeeee(ehh)
string
algae gather
rrruuuh-uuuuhh-(hhh)
grass thick   roots of yellow
flag iris
rrreeeeeeee(ehhh)
males after   rain   late season
bufo incilius   nebulifer
egg strings   trilling long
toad spawn   resonant **uuuuuuhh**
thrummmmming
rainsong rain rut

heretofore

Land Loss 1932–2050

* The Land Loss Between 1932-2000 is historical. The Land Loss Between 2000-2050 is projected based on historical trending if no further action is taken as documented in the "Historical and Projected Coastal Louisiana Land Changes: 1978-2050" (www.lacoast.gov/LandLoss/NewHistoricalLand.pdf)

"As nature teaches us and experience confirms those extracted from a noble blood... are commonly more inclined to honesty than others."

(1565 pamphlet)

J'ai après marcher, ouais, au long de la rivière,

Après échapper de la prison,
Moi j'étais assis là, j'ai arrêté pour me reposer,
Droite là, oui, au long de la rivière.

Hé, la rivière!

—Livaudais 'Les' Sonnier, "Along The River"

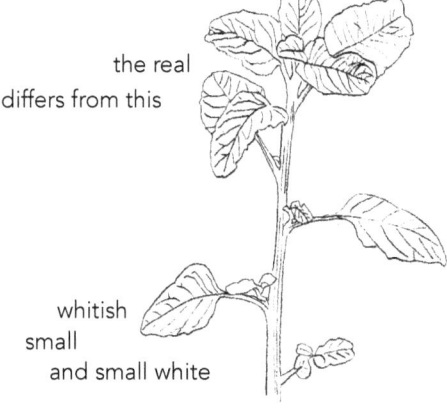

the real
differs from this

whitish
small
and small white

Awakening: Grand Isle

after Kate Chopin

could hear again
the water
the hot south
passed through her
making her eyes burn

the reeds
the salt-water pools
little gray weather-
among the orange
low, drowsy

solitude
flushed and
muddled like wine
a first breath of
the beach

sporadic
acres of chamomile reaching
away still
and lemon trees
the gaunt

water-oaks
the stretch of yellow
melting hazily
blue
water of

the sun
clamoring, murmuring
along the white
up and down
a broken wing

circling
it had no beginning
the sycamore tree

the hum of bees
pinks filled the air

                                                    long, slender

                                                         bending
                                                    black
                                                         taste of almonds
                              used to
                                milk
                                         as
                                       shade
                                      in winter

Chemical Louisiana

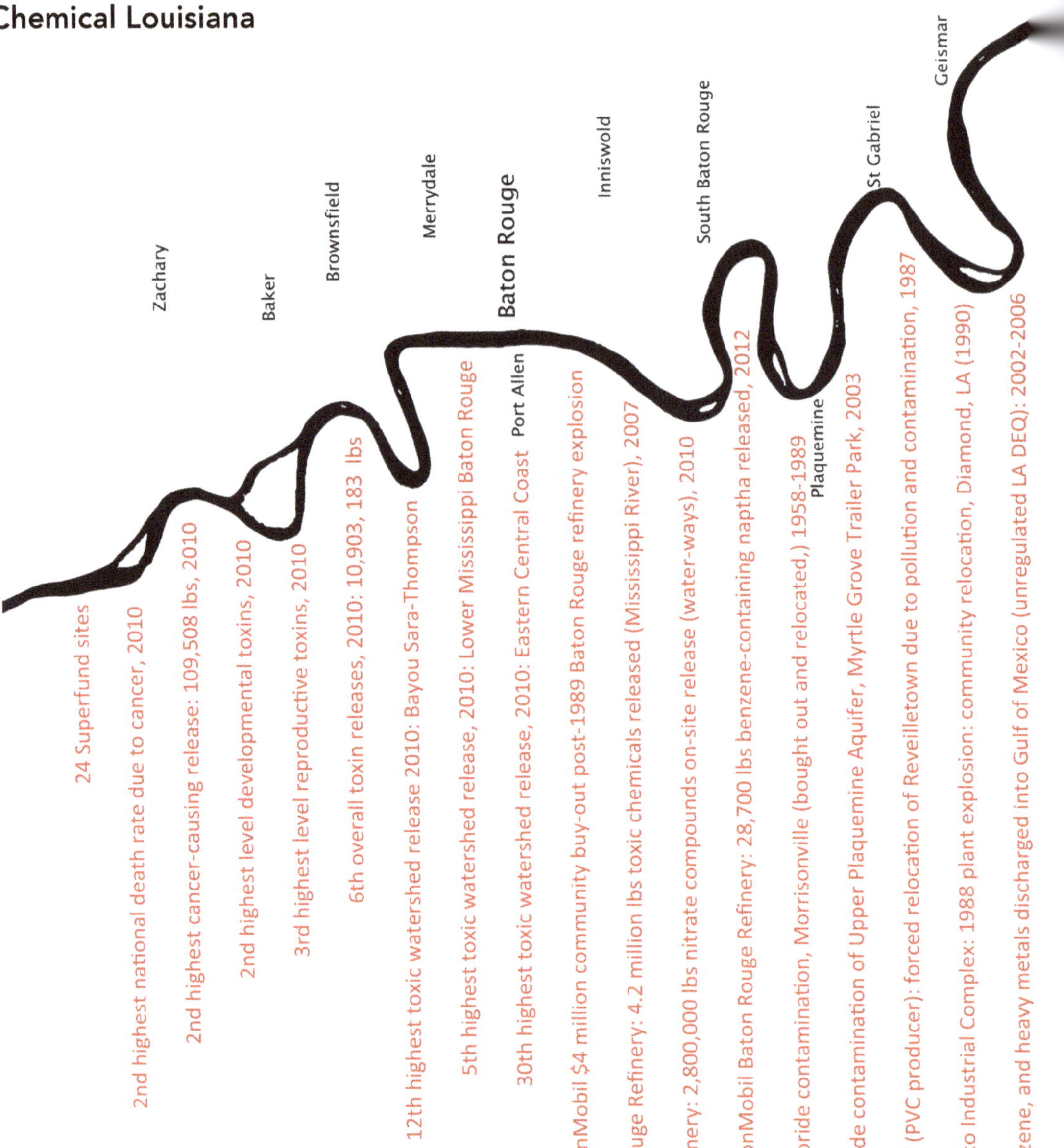
Zachary
Baker
Brownsfield
Merrydale
Baton Rouge
Port Allen
Inniswold
South Baton Rouge
Plaquemine
St Gabriel
Geismar

24 Superfund sites

2nd highest national death rate due to cancer, 2010

2nd highest cancer-causing release: 109,508 lbs, 2010

2nd highest level developmental toxins, 2010

3rd highest level reproductive toxins, 2010

6th overall toxin releases, 2010: 10,903, 183 lbs

12th highest toxic watershed release 2010: Bayou Sara-Thompson

5th highest toxic watershed release, 2010: Lower Mississippi Baton Rouge

30th highest toxic watershed release, 2010: Eastern Central Coast

ExxonMobil $4 million community buy-out post-1989 Baton Rouge refinery explosion

ExxonMobil Baton Rouge Refinery: 4.2 million lbs toxic chemicals released (Mississippi River), 2007

ExxonMobil Baton Rouge Refinery: 2,800,000 lbs nitrate compounds on-site release (water-ways), 2010

ExxonMobil Baton Rouge Refinery: 28,700 lbs benzene-containing naptha released, 2012

Dow Chemical vinyl chloride contamination, Morrisonville (bought out and relocated,) 1958-1989

Dow Chemical vinyl chotoride contamination of Upper Plaquemine Aquifer, Myrtle Grove Trailer Park, 2003

Georgia Gulf (PVC producer): forced relocation of Reveilletown due to pollution and contamination, 1987

Shell Oil Norco Industrial Complex: 1988 plant explosion: community relocation, Diamond, LA (1990)

Oilfield wastewater containing radium, benzene, and heavy metals discharged into Gulf of Mexico (unregulated LA DEQ): 2002-2006

Grand Isle

A friend and I come to Grand Isle in the rain, drive lazily about. Fishing camps and houses on piers dominate the west end post-Katrina, on the east end, a Coast Guard station and a state park. The houses on the marshy side are older, worn-down, sheltered among the oaks of the ancient chenier. Before there was a town, Barataria Plantation sprawled 60 arpents, 2 miles, at the island's widest part. One hundred enslaved people, thirty-eight cabins to house them, a sugar house and machinery. The overseer had his own house, four rooms, outside flanked by pigeonnaires. Levees and a draining machine kept back the Gulf. The plantation owners came to the island for swimming and dinner parties. Amid the ruins, silver spoons and ladles, tablecloths, napkins, fine china for a party of twelve.

During squalls, I sit in the library, high above the ground, watching the Gulf. The librarian brings me books on the history of the island to while away the rain. In *Chita, A Memory of Last Island*, Lafcadio Hearn writes,

> *Southwest, across the pass, gleams beautiful Grand Isle: primitively a wilderness of palmetto (lantanier);—then drained and diked, and cultivated by the Spanish sugarplanters; and now familiar chiefly as a bathing-resort. Since the war the ocean reclaimed its own;—the canefields have degenerated into sandy plains, over which tramways wind to the smooth beach;—the plantation residences have been converted into rustic hotels, and the negro-quarters remodeled into villages of cozy cottages for the reception of guests. But with its imposing groves of oak, its golden wealth of orange-trees, its odorous lanes of oleander, its broad gazing-meadows, yellow-starred with wild chamomile, Grand Isle remains the prettiest island of the Gulf.*

The oak groves are mostly gone, along with palmetto wilderness, meadows, 'quarters,' orange groves, and wild chamomile. Behind the south-facing dunes and stilt-legged cabins, the town offers a handful of restaurants, fishing outfitters, signs for the state park and Coast Guard. On the north side, across Bayou Rigaud, Fifi Island, where pirate Jean Lafitte was rumored to hideout, was largely washed away by Katrina, though some effort has been made to stabilize it. Eastward of Grand Isle, Captain Lafitte also controlled Grand Terre in the early 1900's, a base of operations. In 1834 a military fort was constructed there, ousting the pirate, its ruins still visible from the east end of Grand Isle. Further east, far from sight, lies the remnants of Last Island, Îsle Dernière: a twenty-five-mile-long pleasure ground for the planter class of south Louisiana. Pounded by the 1856 hurricane into two islands, subsequent storms have reduced it to five small islets—East, Trinity, Whiskey, Raccoon, Wine. As with all Louisiana's barrier islands, Katrina caused extensive damage. These islands, along with coastal wetlands, shelter the coast, soaking up storm-surge, their efficacy endangered as the islands and marsh erode.

When the weather clears my friend and I, California natives and beach-starved, walk up and down the shore picking shells. I laugh madly when tiny crabs crawl out of the shells she has stuffed in her pockets, at her mad dance to liberate them. Hearn recalls De Soto's *Espírito Santo* for the sky above the Gulf, its endless reach of blue. Though today rain has made both sea and sky leaden. A two-hour drive from New Orleans—far closer as the crow flies across Barataria Bay—the island remains isolated. In the late 1800's, folk still lived in cottages constructed with bousillage-entre-poiteaux,[28] Creole cottages with long covered galleries, outdoor kitchens and beehive ovens. Still a fishing village, Grand Isle's resident population is only 1,296, though during the annual Tarpon Rodeo it expands by 15,000.

My reverie in the island's library afforded more than history of the island and *Chita*. In the shelves, I also locate *The Blue Book*, a Baedeker for Storyville, New Orleans' red light district, situated in Faubourg Tremé. Within its blue boards, "color" is everything it seems: "white," "octaroon," and "colored" head the lists of women's names. Chiquita Mendez, Mary Prevost, Talie Mosbey—Louisiana's colonial history writ in their names. Prostitution, like slavery, a "peculiar" institution. The Baekdeker carefully assures its readers, "This is the boundary in which the women are compelled to live." Neatly constrained and properly monetized. Adverts offer dinner, cigars, whiskey. Glassware and ozone water—"Nothing better for a HIGH BALL."

A wing of brown pelicans slides over the groin east of the pier, our feet thick with wet sand. The island, the boundary between wet and dry.

[28] Mud and moss between timber framing

grand isle: pat landry

a farmer ‖ knew everybody ‖ French ‖ oystermen by trade ‖ hauling them ‖ heavy sacks ‖ oyster boats ‖ in the summer time

just a place ‖ fish migrated to ‖ barnacles and—‖ a wonderful place ‖ rich soil was real ‖ the first crop in and‖ the French Market in New Orleans ‖ cauliflower, green beans, tomatoes, squash

a sugarcane plantation ‖ when the slaves were ‖ disbanding ‖ big orange orchard just a little strip of marsh‖ last slave cabins ‖ little tourist cabins ‖ and went ‖ to the beach and ‖ a huge hotel ‖ nothing but the finest ‖ the 1893 storm

still ‖ after Betsy ‖ fishing, oyster and shrimping ‖ a fierce storm ‖ '65‖ really a good time what you grew ‖ cows in all them pastures ‖ the lap of ‖ electric lights ‖ was real nice

this was a door ‖ that was a window‖ on Grand Isle ‖ houses ‖ survived everything ‖firm ground‖ good enough over here ‖ blow ‖ or float away‖ with the current

anything ‖ below that ‖ going to get wet

In October 2011, a new shoreline survey was applied to charts 11364 and 11358, and Coast Survey cartographers discovered that several named features no longer existed. Those geographic names were removed from the chart. Additional changes were subsequently made from shoreline surveys that affected chart 11361 and 11364. Those names were also removed from Coast Survey charts and their status was flagged to the U.S. Board on Geographic Names. The following names are retained in official, federal records of the Geographic Names.
  —National Oceanographic and Atmospheric Administration

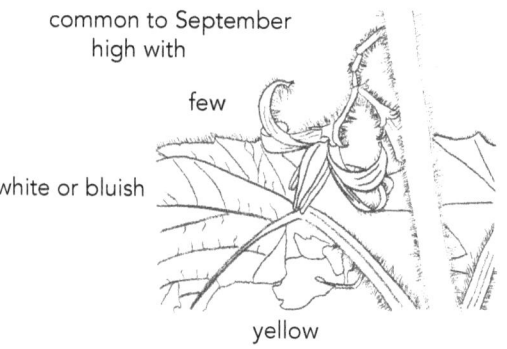

common to September
high with

few

white or bluish

yellow

reckoned a poison

erode || erase

Fleur Pond
Bay Pomme d'Or
Dry Cypress Bayou
Little Bay Pomme d'Or
Skipjack Bay
English Bayou
English Bay
Bay Cheri
Bob Taylors Pond
Scofield Bay
Bay Crapaud
Bayou Auguste
Bayou Long
Drakes Bay
Bay Jacquin
Williams Pass
Bayou Tony
Bayou Caiman
Tom Loar Pass
Pass de Wharf
Little Pass de Wharf
Bayou Petit Liard
Venice Canal
Locust Pond
Andres Pond
Bayou Dum Barr
Cyprian Bay
Yellow Cotton Bay
Grand Bayou Carrion Crow
Bayou la Chute

Réponds: What are the consequences of silence?

    if   nothing

    if   done

          if

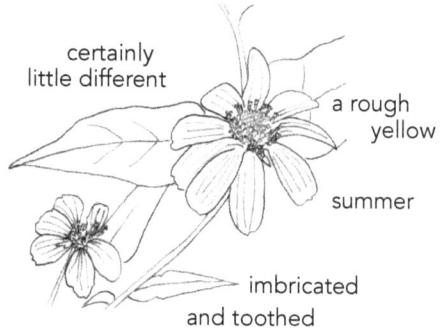

certainly little different

a rough yellow

summer

imbricated and toothed

the remembered place

oneiric
        wind   course   heat   flow

the axis between coast
 and erosion
a comparative lack of limit

      this *intimate space*

felicitous
      set of relations
coast-as-site no
reverie

garden? cemetery?
cross drilling from the floating platform's
umbilical   connections

again and again
thin, slick filler-
cake and cement

seal
the site(s) of entry
less

rigorous
parsing the possible futures

a coast re-
        locates itself
    permeable
margin redefined by salt

              flayed
    torso this

geologically
fluid realm
        nomadic matter
mud knit among weeds

In the bas fonds the oaks of many kinds and the tupelo-gums were hiding all their gray in shimmering green; in these coverts and in the reedy marshes, all the feathered flocks not gone away north were broken into nesting pairs; in the fields, crops were springing almost at the sower's heels; on the prairie pastures, once so vast, now being narrowed so rapidly by the people's thrift, the flocks and herds ate eagerly of the bright new grass, and foals, calves, and lambs stood and staggered on their first legs, while in the dooryards housewives, hens, and mother-geese warned away the puppies and children from downy broods under the shade of the China-trees.
— George Washington Cable, *Bonaventure*

feet high
numerous

hogs are very fond

lettuce and chicory

at Atakapas

Politics

EPA Region 6 Internet Feedback

Original Message: A recent visitor to Barataria Bay, I noted while touring the Bay that only two of the 8 pipes diverting water from the Mississippi were running. I would like to know why only 2 were running, who decides, and how much the other diversion projects in this region are being run: at what rates and how often. The striking difference between the marsh beside the diversion project and the marsh out by Grand Canal Village in Barataria Bay was striking, in terms of the diversity and abundance of plant life as also for animal life. These diversions are essential to protecting and re-establishing the wetlands along the Louisiana coast. Why aren't they running at full power all the time? Thank you for your assistance in this matter.

Marthe Reed

Response by EPA: Thank you for your inquiry regarding the operation of siphons and diversions along the Mississippi River. Regarding the West Point a la Hache siphon in the area you are referring to, Plaquemines Parish operates this and the other siphons in the Parish. The best contact I can provide you regarding siphon operational information in Plaquemines Parish is:

PJ Hahn
Director of Coastal Zone Management
(504) 297-5629
pjhahn@plaqueminesparish.com

In terms of diversions along the Mississippi such as Davis Pond and Caernarvon, I suggest contacting the Louisiana Office of Coastal Protection and Restoration and the best contact I'm aware of is:

Tom Bernard
Louisiana Office of Coastal Protection and Restoration
(504) 280-4071
thomas.bernard@la.gov

I hope these contacts are helpful. Also, as a general strategy, EPA continues to support and propose siphons and diversions as key elements towards coastal restoration.

Paul F. Kaspar
Marine & Coastal Section
U.S. EPA - Region 6
1445 Ross Avenue
Dallas, TX 75202-2733

From: Paul Kaspar (EPA)
To: P J Hahn RE: FYI - Public Inquiry Received by EPA on Diversions/Siphons

P.J.,

FYI - We had received the following inquiry thru our Agency's website regarding operation of siphons & diversions. Just wanted to give you heads-up that I passed your name along as a POC. The response provided to the inquiry is also below. I don't have any background to speak of regarding the genesis of the inquiry, but let me know if you have any questions or concerns.

Paul F. Kaspar
Marine & Coastal Section
U.S. EPA - Region 6
1445 Ross Avenue
Dallas, TX 75202-2733
office: 214-665-7459
mobile: 214-310-6202
fax: 214-665-6689
email: kaspar.paul@epa.gov

FROM: P J Hahn TO: Paul Kaspar (EPA)

CC: Marthe Reed
Krista Clark (Plaquemines Parish)
Blair Rittiner (Plaquemines Parish)
Billy Nungesser (Plaquemines Parish)
Albertine Kimble (Plaquemines Parish)
Lonnie Serpas (Plaquemines Parish)

RE: FYI - Public Inquiry Received by EPA on Diversions/Siphons

Paul, We have two (2) diversions on the west bank of the Mississippi River. Naomi Siphon, which is currently running with three (3) out of the eight (8) pipes open. Unfortunately, the canal needs to be dredged in order for the water to flow more freely. Operating four (4) pipes caused water to backup against the levees, causing concern of compromising our levees along this area. The State has been made aware of the problem, but has not been able to come up with the monies needed to dredge the canal. Ponte a La Hache Siphon is operated through a CEA between Plaquemines and the State. That siphon is currently running (4) pipes out of eight (8), due to construction and repairs to that section of the levees.

Remember that these siphons were designed to regulate the salinity levels in that basin, and are not always running 100% under normal conditions. During high river events, we do monitor salinity levels in this area and adjust the siphons accordingly to maintain a healthy balance. Should you have any further questions, please do not hesitate to call my office.

Regards,

P. J. Hahn Director,
Coastal Zone Management Department
8056 Hwy 23 Suite 307
Belle Chasse, LA 70037

From: Marthe Reed
To: P J Hahn Subject: FYI - Public Inquiry Received by EPA on Diversions/Siphons

Dear Mr. Hahn,

I thank you for your response, though I am surprised to learn that the Parish considers the siphons as only for salinity management in the marsh. Indeed, my correspondence with the EPA in New Orleans made it clear that the EPA sees siphons as vital to coastal restoration. Is coastal restoration via the transport of silt to the basin not a part of Plaquemines Parish policy for dealing with coastal erosion? If so, could you tell me the basis of that policy, as the science indicates that the replenishment of silt to the basin is essential to rebuilding our coastline?

Also, could you tell me why copies of your response to me were cc'd to Mr. Nungasser and other Plaquemines Parish officials? Why would my query be of interest to Mr. Nungasser, unless he is the person in charge of deciding when, how much, and how often the siphons are run? Is Mr. Nungasser, in fact, in charge of making those daily decisions? I had assumed that you were in charge of these decisions. Is this not the case?

Thank you for your time and assistance. I look forward to your response with keen interest and attention,

Marthe Reed

From: P J Hahn
To: Author Name
Subject: FYI - Public Inquiry Received by EPA on Diversions/Siphons

Marthe Reed After reading your response, it is obvious that you have an agenda. I called your office and left you my numbers should you care to discuss this further. As for your comments on who was cc'ed in my email, President Nungesser is the elected leader of our parish and it is my duty to share concerns others have about all aspects of our parish.

Regards,
PJ Hahn

FROM: Marthe Reed
TO: P J Hahn

Subject: FYI - Public Inquiry Received by EPA on Diversions/Siphons

My only agenda is concern for the wetlands and our coastline, which is certainly an agenda. The cc-ing disconcerted me, making me feel that your response was representing an agenda: thus my more pointed response. I felt my question was taken as a challenge, which it is not. I want to understand why what the EPA describes as a project to restore the coastline is described as salinization remediation by the Parish.

I am at home and would be happy to speak with you about this.

Marthe Reed

After this email exchange, I called Mr. Hahn. He was away from his office. When he returned my call, he told me that the diversion projects were all salinization remediation projects, and that fewer siphons were being run due to the need for maintenance or due to Corps' work going on. When I asked about coastal restoration, he cited a study that indicated more land had been lost since silting efforts had begun, though without addressing the impacts oil and gas exploration had over that same period. When Mr. Hahn addressed the oyster bed issue – and salinization remediation as an effort to protect oyster beds – and I asked why oystering had to occur in the newly opened lands, and rather than be re-established in its former locations once the coast was restored, he became unable to hear my questions due to hail and rain lashing his car. I asked him to call me back once he was in his office again. Instead of returning my call, he apparently called Dr. Carolyn Bruder, then Dean of my university, I presume in an attempt to stop the line of questioning I was pursuing.

FROM: Carolyn R Bruder
TO: Marthe Reed Subject: siphon query

Hi, Marthe,

I received a call from an official in Plaquemines Parish regarding an email exchange you all had had on the subject of siphons. He questioned why our university should be challenging their handling of water management. I didn't know what he was talking about, obviously, but apparently you used the "Louisiana.edu" email address, so he perceived your communication as coming from you in your capacity as a faculty member here.

I have no issue at all with your engaging him as a private citizen, but it is probably inappropriate to use the university email account in the exchange since this is not related to your faculty role here.

Thanks for your understanding.

Carolyn

Dr. Carolyn Bruder
Interim Provost and Vice President for Academic Affairs

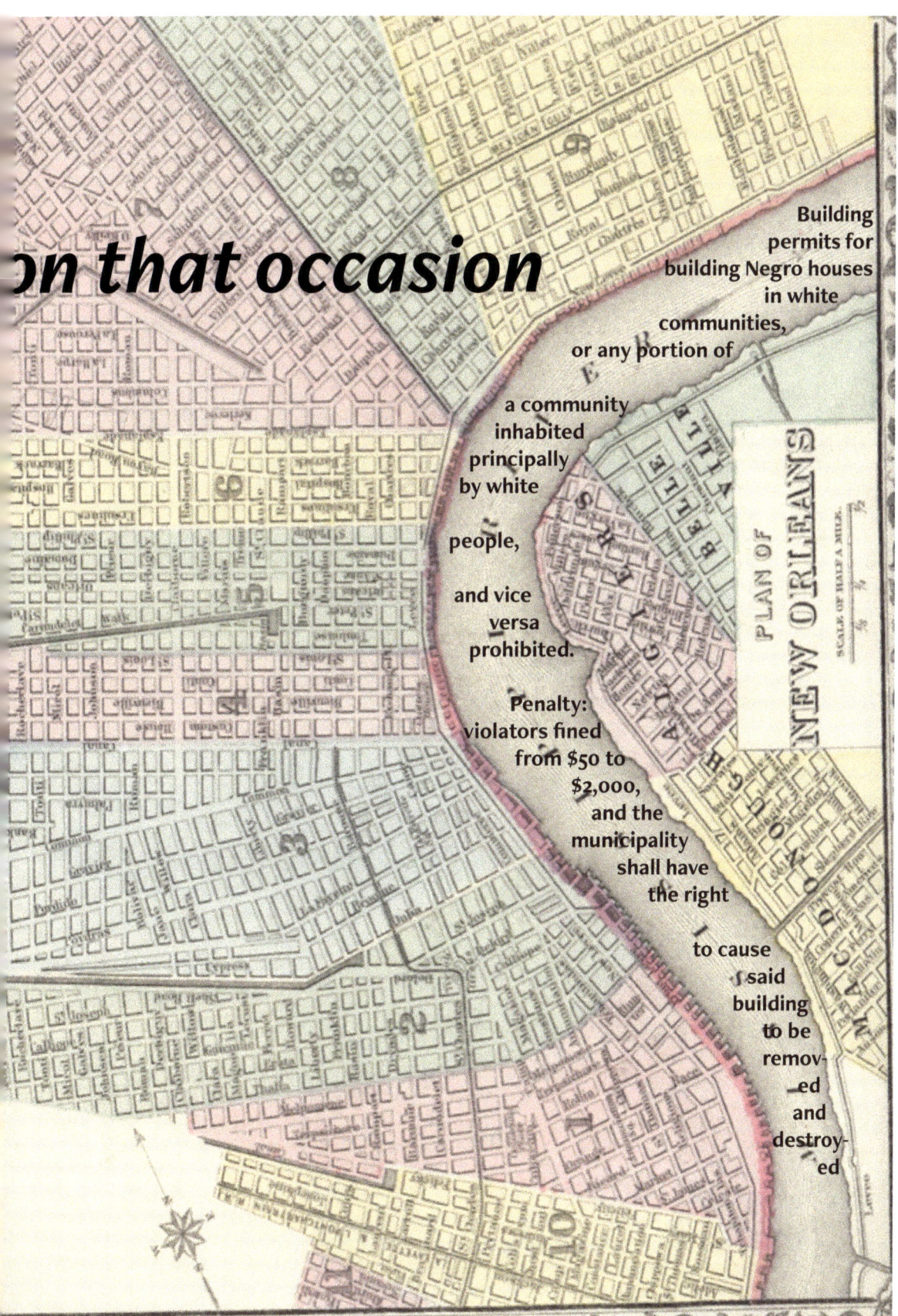

on that occasion

Building permits for building Negro houses in white communities, or any portion of a community inhabited principally by white people, and vice versa prohibited. Penalty: violators fined from $50 to $2,000, and the municipality shall have the right to cause said building to be removed and destroyed

the old city

unrecognizable good this
pure magenta
its lush
roses
populate the old city
recreates it
more mystical
more matter
-of-fact
a glittering wheel turning us
inside out
everywhere
a fabric of abandoned gestures
"Will you be there?"
perilous and not that
being the future
a set of words spelling numerous
attracts her
such vivid exhaustion
"Hurry up!"
coastal geometries sinking into the air
a fundamental circumstance
the bushes flowering furiously
"Well, I—"
sleep's impossible meat

les quartiers

Times are not good here. The city is crumbling into ashes. It has been buried under taxes and frauds and maladministrations so that it has become a study for archaeologists...but it is better to live here in sackcloth and ashes than to own the whole state of Ohio.
—Lafcadio Hearn, letter to a friend, 1879

Binx's Blues[29]

(1)
still burning
sky over Gentilly

it is easily overlooked
strange island

the slightest interest
New Orleans

sags like rotten lace
behind high walls

a week before Mardi Gras
warm wind

and bearing it
the street looks tremendous

devotion
commencing to make a fire

the very sound of winter mornings
streaming with tears

the mantelpiece
an evening gown

against the darkening sky
so pleasant and easy

old world
gone to Natchez

a houseboat on Vermillion
more extraordinary

the sky into
her upturned face

her eyes
a soundless word

ample and mysterious
a litter of summers past

---

[29] Lines excerpted from Walker Percy's *The Moviegoer*

(2)
a fresh wind
transfigures everyone
stray bits and pieces
not distinguishable

a peculiar thing
August sunlight
streaming
in yellow bars

the mystery
of those summer afternoons
the islands in the south
going under

such a comfort
a corner of the wall
enclosed shallow and irregular

the happiest moment
the oddness of it
Carrollton Avenue early in the evening
like a seashell

her fingers on the zinc bar
cold and briney
like a boy who has come into a place
already moved

(3)
inside the wet leaves
the smell of coffee
the Tchoupitoulas docks

Negro men carry children
measuring
the flambeaux bearers

showering sparks
"Ah now!"
maskers

like crusaders
leaning forward
whole bunches of necklaces

that sail
toward us on horseback
loose in the city

the entire neighborhood
possible
somewhere

(4)
simulacrum of a dream
like a sore tooth
commoner than sparrows

celebrating the rites of spring
yellow-cotton smell
thumb-smudge over Chef Menteur

sculling
the bright upper air
the world is all sky

a broken vee
suddenly white
the tilting salient of sunlight

diesel rigs
glowing like rubies
nothing better

evenings
over Elysian Fields
who really wants to listen

in the thick singing darkness
cottonseed
in a streetcar

an accidental repetition
her woman's despair
a little carcass

a kiss on the mouth
not even
the earth has memories of winter

(5)
the sidewalks, anyhow
virginal, as
perfect lawns
fog from the lake

seeing the footprint on the beach
a queer thing
tunneled by
new green shoots

black earth
the very words
full of pretty snapshots

connive with me
down the levee
a drift of honeysuckle
oil cans

forget about women
the sunshine
along her thigh
the tiny fossa

saved me
facet and swell
tilting her head
far away as Eufala

(6)
on Carondelet
we part laughing and dead
a regular little team

easier
two aspirin
a summer afternoon
and the wide sky of Gentilly

come
narrow place
man-smells and
thrush flutings

dry in the
summer's weeds
far flung porches
immaculate

under the streetlight
smell of the hour
when night falls away

(7)
no more than
Judas trees
a sketch of cloud

dreaming
the waters of the sound
the same slow slack

like archeological strata
the difference
rolling in

green and lathered
your heart lifts up
rivulet

tussock of sand and grass
a crown
foams at her knees

thighs asuck
sweeping the water
a sparrow

aslant
the rinsing sadness of it
that yellow dress

lopsided yellow moon
the marsh
cleaves to me

might not see me

(8)
on Bayou des Allemands
a night bittern
like smoke
the boat run into cotton
they've been talking

cleaning redfish
a lap full of
red-wings
cattails
rough boards

voices of the morning
how long it takes
the easy dispensation of the kitchen
blue boat
bayou

black water
aching phosphor colors
Chandeleur Island
like a code tapped through a wall
a habitual disposition

(9)
a drink
a dense pure matrix
swaying against me

blackened and ancient
marvelously high
a moviegoer

as if
all my life
Canal Street

it's blazing flambeau
wheeling
and abstracted

a strange city
aware of us
suppose the right word fails

unnatural metropolis[30]

an unlikely city often I have met[31]
        swamps floods lake river some blooming young man

bilious fevers
and navigational concerns a few hours after

a swath of high ground the black vomit
natural and fiscal inadequacies profuse hemorrhages

        the common disorder
levees expand the capacity of flood mouth nose ears eyes

lower ground, among the poor glistening, yellow
induced the utmost distress

poor drainage stained with blood
yellow jack yellow fever

sewage dumped
along the batture dark, mottled

lapses
        festering livid, swollen

a huge privy the face and whole body
4000 deaths distended

impregnated dusky red
        absolutely poisonous

---

[30] *An Unnatural Metropolis: Wrestling New Orleans from Nature*, Craig E. Colton. Baton Rouge: LSU Press, 2005.
[31] Dr. Clapp, a Presbyterian minister in New Orleans, writing of deathbed scenes due to yellow fever in 1856

When I was a girl the houses were pretty shabby... . And things was pretty lean. And I dunno, I was born into this condition but it was kind of a sad feeling I'd have, 'cause there weren't many of us that lived too well. I had this feeling, I could live better. And I used to dream of living better. But the condition I used to find myself wandering down around the levee, on the other side of the levee near the Mississippi, picking up wood. And my people were poor and I had to draw this wood in that was drifting out on the river up on the sands of the banks of the river and let it dry. And I would take it home that we might have wood for to cook with and to heat with to keep us warm in the wintertime....I would find out on that Mississippi, I would find I could think better. A lot of time I take an ax where there would be old barges laying around and chop wood. It was nothing strange to see a girl chopping wood or cutting down a tree to get kindling for the home. I find a certain joy there...otherwise I'd be sad.
 —Mahalia Jackson, "Recollections of Early Childhood"

rise

and unfold gradually

but sweeter

the only similarity

I don't know any man or woman when I was growing up that did not have a switchblade in their pocket or pocketbook. And I don't remember when I had my first switchblade, but I was definitely a child (laughter). Everyone had switchblades because we needed them; we were being hunted by the police. Anything could go wrong. I was listening to a speech that Ta-Nehisi Coates gave in a Baltimore in a church, and he was talking about how what people don't realize is that black people are afraid. We live our lives often in fear for our physical well-being. And so my father having a switchblade was not only completely normative, but it was smart. And he used it for everything. And my mother had one too, and so did my aunts in their furs and pearls and pocketbooksspeaking of beauty and horror existing simultaneously.

—Robin Coste Lewis

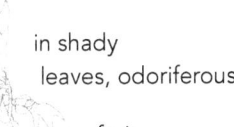

    in shady
        leaves, odoriferous

       fruit
          is excellent
       it never hurts

Vieux Carré

"I wonder why, baby, you want to see me this way."
　　—Robert Pete Williams, "Poor Bob's Blues"

Two of us lean back to back on the levee above the river, night falling about us. Lights limn Gretna Bridge, where town police held the line against Katrina refugees, some trying to get home, some hoping to pass through, some seeking dry land and shelter. Anything preferable to the fetid Superdome, then shots fired over their heads. Here in the Quarter at river's edge, the soft light falling and day cooled down belie that time. Easy sitting here now waiting on nothing much, maybe dinner.

The riverboat glides upriver, calliope silent. Below the levee's shoulder, downtown tourist hotels mount the coastal sky, while across the river, cranes and piers of the port hunker at water's edge. The clamor and jostle of the French Quarter loads the air. Visitors press in clotted lines along Bourbon Street, Royal Street, Chartres, hunting the genuine article, soul of the city to carry home: off-season bead throws, juju, and Saints memorabilia. Visitors stop in for shrimp and andouille jambalaya, gather to-go cups—pink hurricanes spouting straws—the comfort of rum, or beignets thickly dusted in white sugar. The familiar tropes of the city ride like oil on the rocking Gulf. We're done for the day, tired and glad, the vestiges of morning rain gone. Everything but the river seems far off, where we lean among strolling couples, sounds of brass bands welling up from below.

Beyond the tourist bars, mule carriages, and tarot readers of Jackson Square or the hubbub of Bourbon Street lie the wrought iron balconies and bright walls of the Vieux Carré, the city's oldest neighborhood, Mecca of the cool and affluent. Cheek-to-jowl with the Marigny, the Bywater's jazz clubs and pedicabs, and the enclaves of northern migrants in the midst of indigenous poverty, the inhabitants of the Quarter weave tangles of razor-wire over the gates, keep the ground floor windows shuttered tight. At North Rampart Street, the boundary between here and there, the Tremé-Lafitte neighborhood lies in the shadow of Interstate 10. The oldest African American neighborhood in the United States, Faubourg Tremé, Back-o-Town, where Congo Square's diasporic culture and music gave birth to jazz, where Mardi Gras Indians gather on parade days—Pretty Boys fierce and brilliant in their finery—home-ground for the second line. North of Rampart Street, poverty and failed schooling dominate.

East of Tremé are the Seventh and Upper Ninth Wards, across the Industrial Canal, the Lower Ninth. Like the Third Ward west of the Quarter and the CBD, this is the invisible city inside the storied one, where the endgame of centuries of race violence plays out in ruined lives. As with Betsy in '65, Katrina's storm surge flooded through breaches in the Industrial Canal into the Lower Ninth. Still desolated twelve years on, empty lots litter the Lower Ninth. While the rest of New Orleans has returned to close to its pre-hurricane population, the Lower Ninth is nowhere near that. Many from the neighborhood chose not to return, not to rebuild. More than a few of those who did rebuild lost their investment to contractors who never completed the work. Toxic drywall imported from China made matters worse still. New houses in the Lower Ninth lie scattered from one another like fallen teeth. The Make It Right homes, vivid, handsome and surreal in their wildly canted roofs, eccentric shapes, and leggy piers, stand out against the backdrop of isolation. Lovely and strange, alien creatures in a blasted landscape. Wandering through the rebuilt areas, one cannot help but miss the other homes, those half-repaired, their unfinished walls tarped in, tall grass filling in the empty lots, and a sense of pervasive loneliness. While we played tourist among the ruins, hardly anyone was about, the neighborhood resembling a Hollywood backlot more than a place people make their lives. There are no grocery stores and few neighbors. A local non-profit brings in produce for a farmer's market one day a week. The city invested in a senior center: health center, indoor pool, gathering place, a neighborhood in search of a community. The Quarter, however, stayed mainly dry. There the floodwaters reached only the back edge, crossing in from North Rampart where the ground is lower, the original city built on what counts as high ground here.

Upriver from the Vieux Carré, the Marigny and the Bywater have rapidly transformed. The Bywater was once a working-class neighborhood. In this new millennium, its white population has nearly doubled while the black one has been halved. A transformation fed in large part by young people arriving in response to the destruction that befell the city in Katrina's aftermath, this pattern has been exacerbated by young creatives, migrants who fled south to New Orleans after the 2008 crash: artists, musicians, writers, and others, well-educated middle-class seekers after a dream. Their move into affordable Bywater and St. Claude, however, sent rents through the roof. For those who had made these neighborhoods home for generations, home slipped out of reach: no parents back home to make up the difference between what is earned and what is necessary. The former residents were driven further out, often as far as Jefferson Parish in search of rent they could afford. It is a long bus ride into the city for work. And I get it. I, too, am drawn to the Bywater. Jazz at the Bacchanal on a Sunday afternoon in the shade of trees with a bottle of wine, a plate of house-marinated olives, and grilled haloumi cheese is pretty fine, the crowd a mix of longtime residents and newcomers. But then, I'm not trying to live here on $7.50 an hour.

My affection for this city is complicated, unsettled, like so many of my feelings about Louisiana. Neither of this place nor entirely alien to it, here on the levee I occupy the city's strange margins, looking in, looking out—nothing easy. Contingent, ruptured, fervent. Fertile. Against environmental collapse, institutionally structured racism and poverty, against the insidious cynicism of the political class, nevertheless this city exerts its allure on me. The sky burning orange at the end of the day. Trembling prairies like ragged hems of the city's skirts, its margin of error in times of storm. Kosher offerings at Stein's Market and Deli. Handmade pupusas from Macarena's in Carrollton. The strange birds inhabiting the walls of Commander's Palace, the turtle soup served there, the crumbling crypts and ruins of Lafayette Cemetery across the street where best not to wander after dark. The vanished pop-up vegan Korean eatery behind the HiHo Lounge in the Marigny. The sudden joyful sound of a second line coming up the street ("Alright, dig deep, dig deep!"), the community force and pride of Social and Aid Pleasure Clubs, the pothole-filled streets and grubby shoulder-to-shoulder-ness of the city's neighborhoods, the rumbling streetcars along the neutral ground of St. Charles Avenue, the cars' mahogany seats and brass fittings glinting in refurbished splendor. The wide meanders of the river which form the city's edge, that astonishing river bent on its way south. Time eddies here, past, present, and future turning about one another in complicated whorls. A primeval wetland bordering cypress forest, tilled becomes a sugarcane plantation which then gives way to clusters of small farms, to cotton pickeries, breweries, and barrel coopers, to a neighborhood at the edge of the city, becomes finally the Ninth Ward. A band will show up soon, a parade, a crisis. Nothing stops, though we do, the Quarter's noise and light forming an insulating bubble, bauble, around us.

wasted city[34]

Concentrated Disadvantage and Homocide rate coincidence in New Orleans by ward

[34] Homicide data map from *Construction Areas of Homicide Research*

Vast stands of virgin cypress once grew in the swamps and bottomlands of the floodplain, as well as along other rivers and lakes of the area (Viosca, 1928).

by and by

At the time of European colonization, an estimated 11 million to 12 million acres (4.4 to 4.8 million ha) of forested wetlands existed in Louisiana, but by the mid-1970s only about half the original acreage was left. The amount of forested wetlands has continued to dwindle.

Réponds: Describe a morning you woke without fear

        when once
                quondam sea

      mother
to niobram chalk

        shallow   saline
                          slough

    mowrysea ((mowry
                shale)) running

the entire way
    tethys

              sea
  gulf

            f l o o d

    ((before) laramide
hogbacks flatirons thrustfaults

            orogeny)
    when once

when *once*
        north ((   ))

      to south
        seas in flood

  blue gray shale and
            yellow chalk

    p r o f u s i o n

Boat-minded People

Canoeing on Lake Chicot, early enough to avoid April's inexorable heat, we glide beneath low cypress boughs, moving shade to shade. Half submerged tree limbs and trunks clutter the shoreline, water the color of long-steeped tea. Where the canopy opens, turtles sun on logs, snakes in the crotches of trees. A sudden splash reveals an alligator already gone before we can spot it. In the still, humid air, we come with sun hats, water bottles, bare skin, sunblock. Spring in south Louisiana. The thickness of this landscape manifests everywhere. Live oaks coat every surface in chartreuse pollen—houses, cars, patio chairs, the leaves of roses and camellias. Mounds of spent, brown catkins follow. The tumbling narrow leaves, which precede the pollen, crackle over roofs, drives, walkways, mound up where wind is blocked. Here in the swamp, life teems. Flycatchers and gnatcatchers swerve through the air, hunting caddis flies and mosquitos. Herons frog in the shallows. Fishing egrets take wing, glide to roosts in the cypress canopy. Snowy Egrets, Great Egrets, Reddish Egrets, Cattle Egrets. A green heron stands motionless on stocky yellow legs, just at the edge of the wet, waiting on fish. We paddle back into shade, already sticky from mid-morning heat.

Water has always been a way of life in south Louisiana for the Acadian refugees and their Cajun descendants. Crabbing, shrimping, fishing, gathering moss from the swamps, felling cypresses, navigating in hand-hewn pirogues. Commercial shrimping, oystering, and fishing remain important economic activities—a billion-dollar industry—though few folk still live in the wetlands. Oilfield work, however, offered these boat-minded people an unimagined affluence. The oil and gas industry also destroys the landscape on which the fishing industries depend, on which culture and identity hinge: vast networks of ancient cheniers, islands, and wetlands protecting the coast bartered for oil and gas wealth.

Marshes hem the state, secure the silty soil of the coast in their tangled roots. According to the U.S. Geological Survey, 36% of Louisiana's land loss came as a direct effect of the activities of the oil and gas industry and their 10,000 miles of canals through Louisiana's coast. Those canals, routinely abandoned rather than restored as required by state and federal permits, draw the Gulf's salt-laden water inland. When the Southeast Flood Protection Authority sought to sue to hold the oil and gas industries responsible, then-Governor Bobby Jindal fought tooth and nail to protect the interests of oil and gas companies, patrons of his political ambitions, last place in a Presidential primary, race to the bottom. In response to coastal land-loss, 39 suits have been filed against the industry by Jefferson, Plaquemines, and Cameron Parishes, all heavily impacted by wetland loss.

blowout: Melvin Lirette

blowout || out on Vermilion Bay || fought that || forty-two days || that engineer || a mud engineer || son of a gun || pipelines to a little island || big joints || son of a gun || doing that || hear? || Terrebonne Gas || devil horse || shove that || jam it down || turnbuckles to || something wasn't || they || lost an arm || firefighting crew || got killed || that damn four inch || that pack of mud || sack mud || cut off his arm || devil horse || when it blew|| loosen it || they had to loosen it || made a spark

I remember || water lilies || drift by, and oh|| go to pieces || oh, I'm telling you || the derrickman for Texaco || a driller || we pulled out of the hole || right here || the pipe there || pulling out of the hole || a steel plug || that 9 and 5/8 casing || A steel plug || a bum job, cement job || don't know || what the hell || cement job || Halliburton || a bum cement job || in them days || what the hell || to treat mud || a chickenhouse

the derrick || coming out || no weight, light as- || oh god, it come at us || the toolpusher and the roughnecks || an ordinary piece || 1 inch || it blew up || couldn't close it || any other who || a cat in them days || gas blowing through || rope relays || in the barge || jet that || any fire || the damn things || can move || water like that || jetted that || barge out || drilling barge after the blowout

roasted a pig || twenty dollars per family || make it go around || a handful of people || the old seaplane || a bigger plane || the blowout || the boss, the big shot || yeah || on Vermilion Bay || the same time || a Thibodeaux boy || in those days || fish until eight || a little early || a little early || clean the fish || getting ready || getting ready || throwing chain || in the hole

Réponds: Tell me what you know about dismemberment[36]

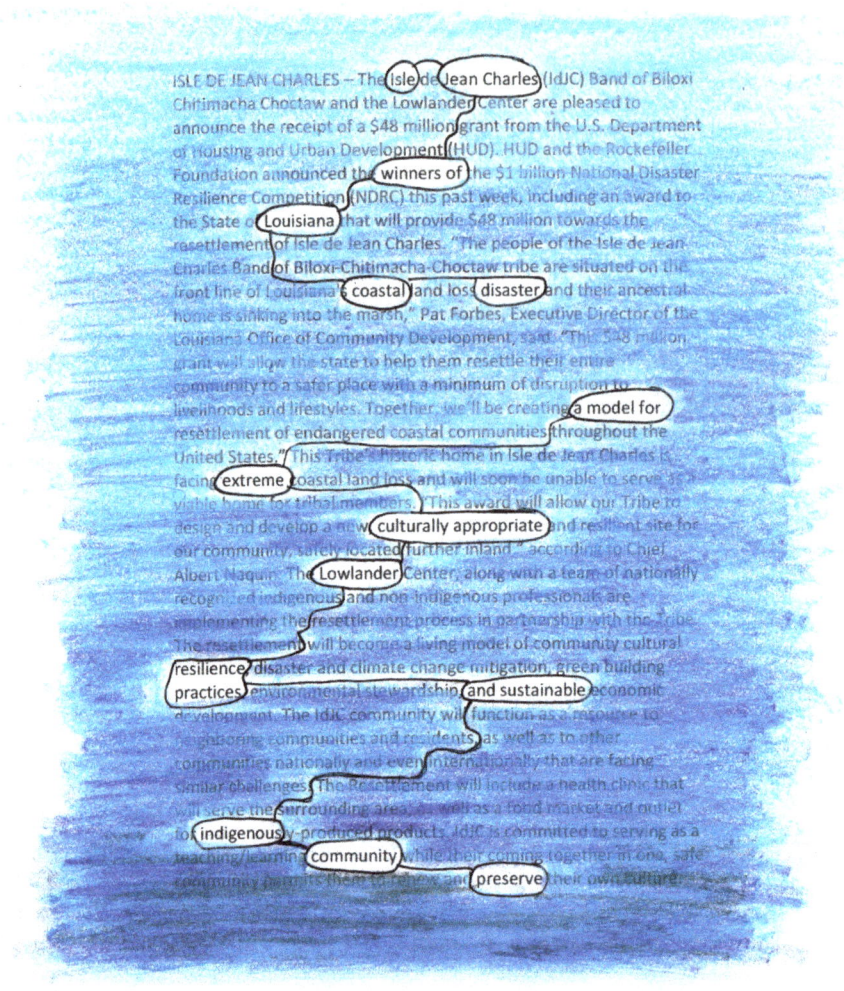

[36] Statement on the Coastal Resettlement website announcing the award of 48 million dollars to the state of Louisiana to resettle the Isle de Jean Charles Band of Biloxi-Chitimacha-Choctaw tribe from their home island to an inland location due to coastal land loss and rising sea levels. http://www.isledejeancharles.com/

Stormtracker[37]

What has happened down here? Is the wind have changed? Clouds roll in from the north and it started to rain. Rained real hard and rained for a real long time. Six feet of water in the streets of Evangeline.
—Randy Newman, "Louisiana 1927"

August 5, 2002 – Tropical Storm Bertha, Slidell, LA
September 5, 2002 – Tropical Storm Fay, Cameron and Grand Isle, LA
September 14, 2002 – Tropical Storm Hanna, Sondheimer, LA

September 26, 2002 – Hurricane Isidore, Grand Isle, LA

October 3, 2002 – Hurricane Lili, Lafayette, LA

June 30, 2003 – Tropical Storm Bill, Chauvin, LA
June 30, 2003 – Tropical Storm Bill, Chauvin and Montegut, LA
August 31, 2003 – Tropical Storm Grace

September 15–16 and September 22-23, 2004 – Hurricane Ivan, Southwest Pass and Holly Beach, LA

October 10, 2004 – Tropical Storm Matthew, Grand Isle and Haynesville, LA

July 5, 2005 – Hurricane Cindy, New Orleans, LA

July 10, 2005 – Hurricane Dennis, New Orleans, LA

August 29, 2005 – Hurricane Katrina, New Orleans, LA

September 24, 2005 – Hurricane Rita, Lake Charles, LA

September 13, 2007 – Hurricane Humberto

September 22, 2007 – Tropical Depression Ten

August 4, 2008 – Tropical Storm Edouard, Cameron Parish, LA

August 31, 2008 – Hurricane Gustav, widespread across the state, 34 parishes declared disaster areas

September 13, 2008 - Hurricane Ike, Morgan City, LA

---

[37] Tropical storms and hurricanes during the eleven-year period during which I was a resident of Louisiana.

November 10, 2009 – Hurricane Ida, Elmer's Island, Grand Island, LA

July 25–26, 2010 –Tropical Storm Bonnie, West Baton Rouge Parish
Mid–August 2010 – Tropical Depression Five

September 4, 2011 – Tropical Storm Lee

June 23–24, 2012 –Tropical Storm Debby, Shell Beach, LA

August 29, 2012 – Hurricane Isaac, St. Bernard, St. Charles, and Lafourche Parishes

Some say tragedy's hard to get over
But sometimes that tragedy means it's over
Soldier, from the academy league of rollers
I deny being down though they seem to hold us
My shoulders are strong I prove 'em wrong
I ain't doing nothing but moving on, let the truth be known
But they talked that freedom at us
And didn't even leave a ladder, damn
              —Lil Wayne, "Tie My Hands"

                                    long and
                                      acrimonious

              a furrow
               fringed

        a raised margin   and

                              three

Wasted

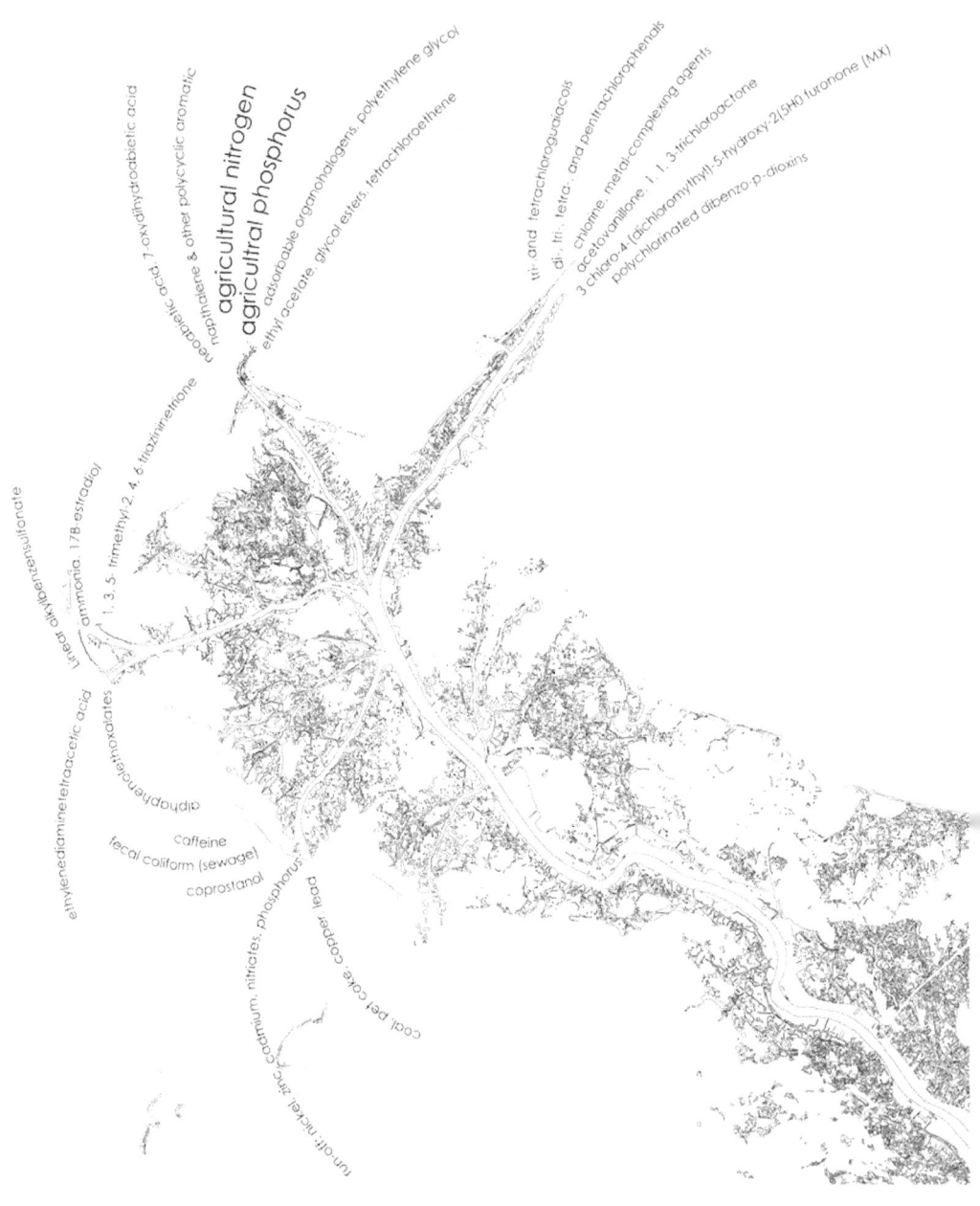

Mapping

Tracing, then labelling, maps affords none of the ease of drawing vines and leaves. I work from printed originals or on an IPad, tracing the intricate lines of coast, river, islands, flow. This is tedious work, zooming in to capture the finer details, then back out and further along, continue the endless line that marks the tentative boundary between water and earth. Off the page, no clear boundary exists, the margin always in flux, tides or boat wake, the ceaseless action of erosion re-staking the line each moment. In winter, the growth of the salt and brackish marshes slows nearly to a stop. The browning vegetation becoming next season's soil, the seeds of the rushes feed migrating waterfowl. Spike-rush and widgeon grass, coco and three-cornered grass. In spring brown shrimp make these marshes a nursery. Later mottled ducks mate and hatch their broods amid the wet. The seed-heads form in summer when salinity rises, when white shrimp arrive to clutch. Teal ducks come in late summer, while alligators guard their young from other alligators' predation. In autumn the white shrimp mature and head Gulfwards, and marsh mosquitos hatch, once the traditional season for trapping nutria and muskrats.

I come to Cocodrie in early summer to visit LUMCON, Louisiana Universities Marine Consortium, and am astonished by the lush green of the marsh as I walk over the floating boardwalks. At the Research Station, scientists from around the country study the impacts of the BP Horizon oil catastrophe on Louisiana's coastal ecosystems, the toxins leached through marsh grass, crustaceans, sea mammals and birds, and terrestrial birds. Back at home, the view is less spectacular, the research a matter of sifting the internet: agricultural nitrogen and phosphorus run-off spiking a dead-zone in the Gulf, the movement of industrial toxins, sewage, and pharmacological waste through the outlets of the bird-foot delta, the history of industrial spills along the Mississippi, identifying the names of lost bodies of water in Barataria Bay, or marking the co-incidence of "concentrated disadvantage" and homicide in New Orleans. The maps take a steady hand, returning again and again to trace the lines, as if I might somehow mark centuries of suffering and harm carved through this landscape. Do the names of New Orleans' wards give a shape to that history? How do I know where I am?

oilfield dreams: roy champagne

why don't you come
rough-necked
pushin' tools
drilling rigs oddly anywhere

intimate and far
flung that deep slow
going all the time
a decent life

specific bodies in
specific places
a bar and a grocery store
Cut Off

and my brother
all south
marsh then bays
nice big rigs

further out
back back of
Napoleon Bay
Ponchartrain Southeast

Pass
mud drillpipe
between them rigs
casing

never slowed down
a rope
a jack-up a steady
risks lie across

a yellow sheet
that
grandfather clause
water fuel mud

check
a transparent reality
three thousand
sacks those connections

class-A
cement

the world drowned
you all feel all feel

ten foot seas
to kill
that white yellow and red
systemic and irreversible

mud
comes yellow
too late
neither culpability nor

solutions
a breakdown
a blow-out same thing
you're gone

Dead Waste

"The next summer, 1794, corn grew dear, and distress began in our land."
—Joanna Southcott

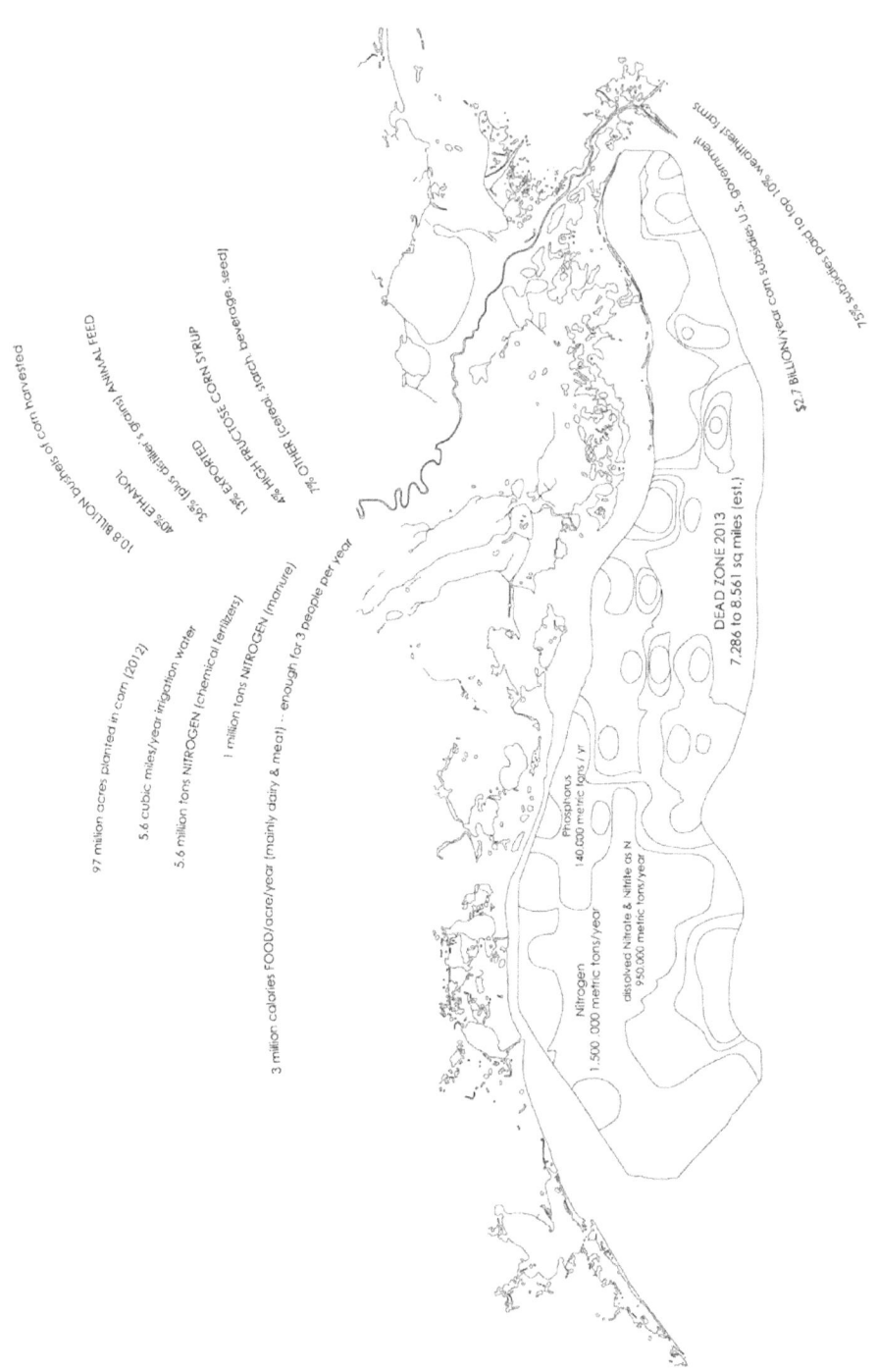

Réponds: How will you live now?

amphibian double-lunged
    ((geographer))

        permeable
                wet

    thickair
            hyacinth-and-lotus

    ((hallucinatory

        (body)))

    garden ::

      branching vines
collate   light

  thinscaled

      spanish moss

  ((memory))   chronology

sutured bowl

    Omne vivum ex vivo

((generation))

      softashyacinth this

((body) like)
      any weed

                    carex sedge   and cypress
                          anchor   intuition

       ((duckweed))
finger root   tangle

      Casmerodius albus   consummate
fisher ::   vegetal anatomy

                soak gleams ::
   torso (( )) tenement   matter d i l a t e s

                    drowses

             aero
naut yellow legs black

                    ((body)   saturated air
bill diffused in green

      mangrove   aerial rootwork
           respiration

            arrru(p)   arrru(p)   aarrru(p)

The changes men have made in Southern Louisiana these last few years are great. I say nothing, again, of the vast widths of prairie stripped of the herds and turned into corn and cane fields: when I came, a few months ago, to that station on Morgan's Louisiana and Texas Railroad where Claude first went aboard a railway-train, somebody had actually moved the bayou, the swamp, and the prairie apart! —George Washington Cable, "The Shaking Prairie"

Les 'Cadiens

Hybrid realm, wet and dry, woods and fields: South Louisiana was settled by people from many cultures. After the Atakapas-Ishak, Chitimacha, Choctaw, Houma, Coasati, and Tunica-Biloxi, the French and Spanish came. Creoles. Les Acadiens. Bourbons and Isleños. Italians, Germans. Cajuns and Coon Asses. Czechs, Hungarians, Jews, Croatians, Filipinos, Mexicans, Cubans,

Guatemalans, Chinese, Vietnamese, Laotians, Thais. Waves and waves of migrants. Lac des Allemands. Manila Town. Bon Secour, Catahoula, Caernarvon, Calcasieu, Bogue Falaya, Brittany, Caspiana. Mixed, multiple. Many. In Acadiana, those who took up the life-way of the Cajuns became Cajun also, French surname or no. Cajun family names such as Schexnayder, Reed, McGee, Romero and Waguespack are not uncommon among more obvious French names like Breaux, Broussard, Boudreaux, Thibodeaux.

Married in a shared way of life founded in fresh seafood and the home-grown or made: etouffé, filé gumbo, oysters on the half-shell, andouille sausage, red beans and rice, a paradise of fried food. Oyster po'boys, shrimp po'boys, catfish po'boys, soft shell crab po'boys. Soft French bread rolls and mayonnaise. Hot sauce. A bottle of NOLA Blond and a table in the shade. Spicy crawfish or crab boil turned out upon a newspaper-covered table.

And a love of porch music, dance music. A friend and I drive toward Breaux Bridge to breakfast at Café des Amis. Along the road, a mile or so from town, we pass a Zydeco trail-ride heading the opposite direction. Men and boys on bays, browns, and paints, western saddles, cowboy hats and boots, young kids riding in front of dad or pops. Headed to a picnic and to play music, the riders laugh, settling skittish horses, waving a beer in their free hands. Up ahead, pickups haul trailers loaded with families and coolers, one ferries the DJ blaring Zydeco, dance time, syncopated time, leading the way. Families gathering or communities, the trail-rides have their origins in Creole cowboys working cattle in Louisiana and Texas. At the end of the trail-ride, folks will feast on barbecue, gumbo, cochon de lait while the frottoir and accordion pull everyone to their feet. I know when we get to breakfast, the band will already be playing and someone will ask me to dance, step slow-quick-quick.

threnody

waiting it out, we might as well
forgive the loan
sorrows stacked like cordwood
under the stair, sow's heart beating

at a closer angle, the water's ink
becomes translucent
breaking the surface
and the horizon flips

I push through a maze of dry
lotus pods, rattled and brash
distance erodes with the trees t
hough everything is up for discussion

the action unfolds off-stage
a rancid aftertaste
devoid of future
a habit of water and erosion

inevitable as the terms of the contract
tucked into an opposite moment
rising gulf headed north
then no longer exists

the slow pulse of tidal force
I am growing into myself
moss leaf twig stem
adrift on the wake

Bayou Corne incident

Ah, well, et ça semble vrai, tout ça, vous comprends?
—Wilson "Ben" Guinē Mitchell

cess pool mud pool sink
extractive detritus
sparkles invisibly from its depths
radium thorium potassium TENORM

orange tongue and blue fire
earth bubbles open
escape velocity of gas under
                              pressure

somewhere at the arcane political desk
this year next year
any of their decay products
a nuclear memo ((DNR))

Department of Natural Resources
gas rattles the earth
radium 226 228 radon
salt mud sink Bayou Corne spewing

methane hydrogen-
sulfide carbon-
dioxide ethane propane pentane butane
a whole biogenic

thermagenic scheme
keeping it under
wraps
Louisiana DNR (do not report do not

respond) "and
asked for patience"
tout ça radionuclides pumped into
Texas Brine™ "surprised as

anyone"
radioactive dome
"slurry area"
expanding 16,000 sq ft mire

the specific gravity of memos
bottom lines "no
detection" of radiation
was discovered

a failed
ça semble vrai integrity test
gas breaching the salt
boundary

radioactive scale
concentrated as a result of
risk calculations and
industrial processes :: radio

-active scale transport models
veneer cavern walls
salt   dome
salt

reservoir not yet tested
subsidence and sub
        surface instability
the possible state of

emergence "never
anticipated"
accumulation
collapse Texas Brine™

"kind of shocked" DNR
authorized disposal
"might be related to…"
naturally

occurring radio
-active material NORM
"…structural problems in the cavern"
a completely

arbitrary distinction
"a relationship to
what was going on"
technically enhanced

tremors and gas bubbles
thorium series decay
crude oil refinery wastes
for weeks

"imagine…" first
instability of cavern reported
20 months earlier
DNR

department of naturally occurring
resistance the best
practices
business practices oil and

eying the bottom
line a *positive business
climate* gas production
"…our surprise"

vous comprends?
150 homes evacuated
2.5 acres become 35
and growing

Texas Brine™
burning off
40 million cubic
feet of escaping gas

"I don't think
anyone could see this coming"

Catechism

A nomadic wanderer following the trajectory of my partner's academic career, intimate connections to place have moored me in response to re-locations half-way round the world and back. After seven years in Western Australia, we came home, landing in Lafayette. The aridity of Australia's ancient continent, landscape of desert and stone, acacias and eucalypts, contrasts acutely to the lush verdancy of Louisiana. These bottomland forests, wetlands, and prairies, Louisiana's tangled history and cultures unsettled and astonished me. Here, nothing was hard, firm, solid, sure. Only drift, compression, flood, silt. Writer Bhanu Kapil's twelve questions, 38 posed to diasporic Indian women she met in her travels—voices of displacement, alienation, and return, wanderers turning toward a home far from everything familiar—offered a pivotal opening into this new country in which I found myself starting over again.

How will you begin?

What is the shape of your body?

Describe a morning you woke without fear.

If south Louisiana, if a gathering of such peoples and histories, the vast movements of earth water, weather, and ecosystems, could speak, what would those manifold presences disclose?

Where do you come from/how did you arrive?

Rock-mountain-erosion-flood.

Water, silt, salt, clay.

Brackish and sweet. One sea given way to another.

Tell me what you know about dismemberment.

Pipeline and canal thresh, dredge and drudge, gas flaring into the cloud-lit night, fiery blowout blackening day. Corpse garden, plague hollow, hurricane watch. Tornado watch.

Flood waters spill over the banks of the levees.

Describe a morning without fear.

Palimpsest of deluge and silt, standing in plain sight, bared fact and bare roots defying cultivation. Mutable as the weather, heavy and wet.

What are the consequences of silence?

---

[38] *The Vertical Interrogation of Strangers* (Kelsey Street Press, 2001).

What would you say if you could?

Put spade in and dig.

The messy carnage of present-past, past-present—weeds and tilth: geological histories, accident reports, Environmental Protection Agency assessments; documentation of early European encounters with the Indigenous peoples, of African enslavement, the German Coast Uprising, the Civil War in Lafayette; studies of pollutants and run-off into the Mississippi River and Gulf of Mexico, oil and gas extraction's destabilization of the coast; oral histories, autobiographies, memoirs, stories, tales; Social Aid and Pleasure Clubs, Mardi Gras, Second Lines; dance halls and jazz clubs, foodways and Jim Crow.

Finding my way by means of books, archives, the living world—trekking, talking, gathering, listening—I compile a record of my passage, seeking answers to Kapil's and my own questions. Sediment core sample. Choral fugue. Quilt, songbook, archive. No single metaphor suffices: like pelicans over the shore-break, gliding, diving, heading away, I hunt fragments amid the froth and dross of the tides. *Where am I now? What does it mean to be here?*

Texas Brine Company, LLC

UPDATE August 14, 2012

                                      any hydrocarbon

                                                                                  on the surface
       water   a path
               a long boom

                                                              plan for

observation

                                                                     drilling
                                                escorts   rig

      components

                                                       2-3 days

                                                                    evacuation

UPDATE August 18, 2012

                     assembled and
             expected

observation
        assistance checks
                                          123

                                          going

           other matters

                                                virtually unchanged

               an effort to   remain in
                  place
      sinkhole   resumption

UPDATE: August 27, 2012

                                              suspended   anticipation
     Isaac's   path across

                     secure   as
                                            drilling
        will evacuate

 sinkhole   all air and
            equipment
                       have departed   day

UPDATE September 6, 2012

     casing
               a diagonal   salt dome
                    afternoon

       sinkhole

                 aerial survey
                                  radiation

  methane or

       chemical   plumes
    found no
          or near cavern
 elsewhere

UPDATE September 30, 2012

    No additional   available   interior
    No additional   available   condition

UPDATE October 15, 2012

        plans for

                Hydrocarbon removal
      review

     no observable
            trees
leaning

          north
    deployed to   contain   access by recovery

UPDATE October 26, 2012

    liquid hydrocarbon   remains in
         cavern
                    well casing
   shut in
           no observable
 removal   No pressure

     aquifer   not expected

UPDATE November 6, 2012

         remained shut
   no reported   debris
      sloughing
       liquid hydrocarbon
surface

   natural gas

            flaring   nonstop
    a steady 14 p.s.i
            forward

UPDATE November 25, 2012

        shut in and

                monitor
  no observable

 caprock   remains shut in
     another   plan   a new

well   placed

    remains shut in
 excess water   inside
        and   expected venting

resume

UPDATE December 9, 2012

        shut in
         natural   and liquid hydro
          the possible   hydrogen sulfide

 revealed   bubbling in
                   debris
    no clean-up
      secured in   perimeter
     "geophone"

           system array
 natural gas
       36,000 cubic

    well   flow rates. Flaring will
  no work   shallow aquifer
monitoring
     begin   cleaning   flushing
 Bayou Corne
     gas zone   deeper
                begin

UPDATE December 29, 2012

        remain closed
                          early   no observable
  sinkhole   no clean-up
            monitored

  natural gas
    23,000 cubic feet   safely   shut in ane
No assessments

      in-home   monitors
            pipeline   right-of-
  monitored   pressure in   aquifer

                                certain seismic
  real-time   data

sudden sun

    sudden sun
        warming   in   two dimensions
                here ||

now   thin cloud-line
      frozen   ((artemisa

                in blue
       ((absinthe   mid-February
                       in blue

    spring   waits
sudden weight of warm air ::
  ((sweet
      at its edge

             mockingbird chjjjjjj
                    ((fennel
        day   shimmering

  plays itself into
       existence   ((green
                  anise

       frostburned hyacinth
          like chronology   ((gin   mutters

    late winter's hydrological talk

threnody

wind measured as
movement
through a live oak's limbs

gray branched body
tossed green
against what seems

nothing
at all
a form of memory

what we ask
one another
cultivating time

leaf clatter rising in
morning sun's
urgency

blue jays
brown thrashers
parasitic ferns

morning
displacements
twist into light

warm water's
melancholy weather
like an afterimage of rain

where I find myself
bruised awake
giving way

Réponds: And what would you say if you could?[39]

purplish, every one

    a fine, thick

        rose

and all the following

        along the rivers

Curages

        smell like honey

plenty

to the bees

[39] Language excerpted from *Florula Ludoviciana*, entry for Smartweed.

after-words

ACKNOWLEDGMENTS

Gratitude to the following journals and anthologies for publishing excerpts (or versions thereof) from *Ark Hive*: *The Volta* "Trash Issue," *Jacket2* "Poems and Poetics," *Otoliths, Marsh Hawk Review, Entropy, Loose Change, Unlikely Stories, horse less review, Ottowater, The Dusie Kollektiv, Poets for Living Waters, The Gulfstream: Poems of the Gulf Coast, Lit of Our Climes, The Arcadia Project, Tupelo Quarterly,* and *BAX 2014*.

The poems titled "Réponds" take as instigation Bhanu Kapil's questions in *The Vertical Interrogation of Strangers*.

Gratitude also to the University of Louisiana Library's Louisiana Room for access to oral histories of oilfield workers, and for the support of the university and English Department during my tenure there.

Deepest gratitude to dear friends, the poets who read and nudged and suggested turns that led to the form this book has taken: Laura Mullen, Eileen Tabios, and Brenda Iijima, and to the summer workshop at Naropa with Eleni Sikelianos where the many of the ideas percolated and grew.

AN ACTIVE ACKNOWLEDGEMENT :: REFLECTIONS ON ARK HIVE
BRENDA IIJIMA

Ark Hive is a broadly conceived, interrelational meditation on human and other-than-human social-cultural realities within place, focused on southern Louisiana, documented in the midst of spiraling ecological and social devastation. At once personal--a memoir, this book is also an incredibly open and inclusive matrix of interwoven contemporaneous and historical forces. In an email to me, Marthe stated that the C.D. Wright quote that serves as an epigraph was the impetus of *Ark Hive*: *However briefly I find myself in a strange place, I am intent on locating myself; where I came from at this point is portable; I carry it with me.* Marthe worked on the text and graphics that make up this book while living in Lafayette for eleven years with her family, "a period stretching from Hurricane Lily through most of Governor Bobby Jindal's tenure as governor"--is how she expressed the timeline.

As if documented in an all-weather geological field notebook in plein air, within elemental concern and total ecological bearing, *Ark Hive* touches upon geologic and biospheric transformation as well as the social and cultural changes that occur simultaneously to a place, a home, a region: an ecosystem of living presences. "A piece of land is always a form of collectively living a territory, a form of inhabiting it, caring for it and protecting it as if the body itself were its extension." Marthe categorizes the book as a memoir of South Louisiana--the of[1] and about that sustains and destabilizes the residents of this region including she and her family and the region itself, an integral point in the web of life. The nucleus of the book is Louisiana, a parcel of land and a brimming ecology that continues to carry a name demarcated by French colonial settlers who took possession of the lower Mississippi region, naming it after their sovereign, Louis XIV, King of France who reigned from 1643 to 1715. The text and graphics telescopes and focuses, bringing in wideranged and micro detail. Central to the narrative is an acknowledgement of the colonial-settler legacy of the decimation of Indigenous people and appropriation of their homelands. *Ark Hive* is as much a book about resilience as Louisiana continues to be home for Native Americans including the Akakapa, the Opelousas, the Caddo, the Natchitoches, the Chitimacha, the Choctaw, the Houma, the Natchez, the Taensa and Avoyel, and the Tunica, as well as the indigenous communities who were driven into Louisiana after the Europeans arrived including the Alabama, the Biloxi, the Konsati and Coushatta, and the Ofo. With rebellious anti-imperial energy that speaks truth to power, Marthe traces the history of slaves and slavers, connecting the racist present to the racist past, placing white supremacy under scrutiny in all its guises. Louisiana, until 2018, held the dubious distinction of incarcerating more people than any other state (in the country that holds the record for imprisoning more of its population than any other nation on earth), racial disparity running rampant, blatant racial targeting in for-profit prisons.

---

1   Liasons, *In The Name of The People*, p. 47

Ark Hive is a record of the potent legacy of[2] freedom fighters--civil rights activists past and present whose contributions have changed the way national and community life is imagined. Black Lives Matter activist Bree Newsome's courageous act of taking down a Confederate flag from the South Carolina statehouse grounds is an impetus for the removal of all Confederate monuments in New Orleans.

Historical and real-time human affairs are everpresently situated within ecological reality: flora, fauna, mineral, water, earth, air. The Mississippi courses through, as do the many waterways of the region. Spillover, run-off, absorption; pathways and circulatory routes within ecosystem, economic zone and the cultural imagination.

>   "palimpsestic language and history--
>   damp, bird-foot, opossum, batture
>   a translation, articulating experience
>   one into an(other)
>   placeMound
>   Builders, slavers, French
>   colony the wet
> whispers its own arguments
> over my skin, irrefutable
>
>   *topos*   the relation between
>   local particulars and
>   human inhabitants
>   a world defined by language
>   Teche   Arcady   Natchez
>   Pontchartrain   Tangipahoa
>   its surfaces collaborate
>   hybrid, synthetic"[3]

The title of this epic work is composed of two words that reverberate when placed side by side: ark and hive. Together they sound out 'archive'. Historically, archives are highly safeguarded collections of documents deemed by a power elite to be of value and essential in the continuance and furtherance of their dominance and myths of superiority. Marthe performs a reckoning with archive. She opens up points in the archive that have systematically diminished and or erased the importance and impact of gender, race and class as well as ecological presence. Indigenous living history takes precedence over colonial mythmaking and obfuscation. With a hive mind, she accumulated and assembled experiential data from diversified sources that give rise to a holism. Complex multiplicity is consequential. References tangle, binding together the missing importance of persons occluded from the record. The ark, a floating vessel, is the vehicle that echoes the mobility of the facts of persons' lives held down, misidentified and mistaken. The hive is her metaphor

---

2   http://www.sentencingproject.org/publications/color-of-justice-racial-and-ethnic-disparity-in-state-prisons/ ; III. The Scale of Disparity

3   ARK HIVE, p. 30.

for communal responsiveness and interaction. We hear the polyphonous effect of myriad voicings. Life proliferates within the *Ark Hive*. Marthe, the poet, citizen, activist (she was a passionate feminist allied with LGBTQ rights and advocate for environmental and racial justice) is always among others, always keenly focused on the concerns and demands that make justice possible. "Voices of the morning/how long it takes the easy dispensation of the kitchen/blue boat bayou"[4]

Contemplating the role of the female archivist steering the ark through and eventually out of his-story is so satisfying. It seems the case that the catastrophe that is capitalism, that has been the reason for unending war and exploitation and has excited forth global climate change is the accelerant that demolishes history--its history of ownership. The narcissism of history (its stories and glorifications of profiteering, exploitation and appropriation) is its own worst enemy. Marthe, with mature knowledge of earthly vulnerability, guided her senses through stages of demise and at every turn, found ways to recuperate meaning, validity and a generosity of connectivity through one-on-one and communal action. A major paradigm shift is initiated just by the fact that *Ark Hive* is an emphatically inclusive document. She has included the rich floral community within the body of this work, thus bringing the equity of attention to the living, breathing sentience of 80 percent of the Earth's biomass: plants. Plants have existed at the bottom of a[5] psychic hierarchy. Their instrumentalization has systematically backgrounded plants as passive and inert beings not worthy of consideration or care. It is a blatant assertion, and still rings true, that flora continues to be gendered female, and therefore deemed less important on the hierarchy of life forms in Western cultures. Flora slips out of human consciousness and an especially major oversight takes place in the Genesis flood narrative when "God instructs Noah to collect specimens of living creatures, which will be able to repopulate the Earth once the flood has receded. In the context of this rescue job, however, plants are not designated as living beings. Therefore, not a single individual from the world's three hundred thousand flowering plant species is taken onto the ark." The ark is said to have been fabricated out of gopher[6] wood, another name for cypress. The majority of Southern Louisiana's sprawling cypress swamps were clear cut nearly a century ago to make for burgeoning human development, and the practice of razing swamps of stands of cypress continues, their trunks ground down into wood chips, and other disposable products.

Marthe rectifies the ontological split that exists between plants, animals and humans in the Western, Judeo-Christian tradition. Plants are given major consideration in this work. Plants are understood as conscious, active, self-directed, sentient, communicative, interactive: able to act collectively and autonomously, have feelings, have familial connections, experience dying and death and also thriving. *Ark Hive* advocates for

4   *ibid*, p. 124.
5   https://www.smithsonianmag.com/smart-news/humans-make-110000th-earths-biomass-180969141/
6   Matthew Hall, *Plants as People, A Philosophical Botany*. SUNY Press, 2011, p. 59.

human-floral relationships that are ecologically appropriate, ethical and take into consideration the personhood of plants. *Ark Hive* abounds in plant presences dialogically storying the book. Plant intelligence is keen, "with thousands of meristems, a plant has potentially thousands of 'brain units'. It is proposed by advocates of plant neurobiology that plants integrate sensory information and make decisions based upon communications between a multiple of plant tissues such as the root, meristems, internal meristems, and the vascular tissues."[7]

Ark Hive processes grief through the intertwined realms of the aesthetic, the ethical, and the political as they play out across bodies (human and non-human) in both mundane and extraordinary ways. Grieving passes through many stages as an active process of the acknowledgement of sorrow and loss. "Time eddies here, past, present, and future turning about one another in complicated whorls." p. 138. Within the moving objects of attention that make these poems there is an expression of the continual shouldering of grief, and also a commitment to easing the grief of others." Marthe experienced the 2010 Deepwater Horizon catastrophe while living in Louisiana. The Deepwater Horizon oil spill is recognized as the worst oil spill in U.S. history. "By the time the well was capped on July 15, 2010 (87 days later), an estimated 3.19 million barrels of oil had leaked into the Gulf. In the case of the Deepwater Horizon oil spill, clean-up workers treated the oil with over 1.4 million gallons of various chemical dispersants." For microscopic[8] animals living in the Gulf, even worse than the toxic oil released during the 2010 Deepwater Horizon disaster may be the very oil dispersants used to clean it up, a new study finds."[9] Coursing throughout are other intersecting catastrophes and the disproportional effects they have on communities of color and those disenfranchised economically and for other reasons.

Documented are the shifting balances of an ecosystem in her vicinity experiencing ruination. Marthe understood the Deepwater Horizon event as a yet another disaster, compounding precarity, contingency, and crisis. These actualities are organized in a way that the micro informs the macro and vise versa, as do the geologic and historic past and the momentary present. Southern Louisiana signals what human engineered ecological collapse looks like in our present moment. The US has already been stripped of half of its wetlands since Europeans arrived and Louisiana, which accounts for a bulk of these losses, is on course to lose all of its wetland within two more centuries, according to the US Geological Survey "The southern coast of Louisiana in the United States is among the fastest-disappearing areas in the world."[10]

This has largely resulted from human mismanagement of the coast. At one time, the land was added to when spring floods from the Mississippi River

---

7   *ibid*, p. 148
8   https://ocean.si.edu/conservation/pollution/gulf-oil-spill
9   https://www.mnn.com/earth-matters/wilderness-resources/stories/dispersant-makes-oil-52-times-more-toxic
10   https://pubs.usgs.gov/fs/la-wetlands/

added sediment and stimulated marsh growth; the land is now shrinking. There are multiple causes. Artificial levees block spring flood water that would bring fresh water and sediment to marshes. Swamps have been extensively logged, leaving canals and ditches that allow saline water to move inland. Canals dug for the oil and gas industry also allow storms to move sea water inland, where it damages swamps and marshes. Rising sea waters have exacerbated the problem. Some researchers estimate that the state is losing a land mass equivalent to 30 football fields every day." The National Oceanic and Atmospheric Administration had to remap the nearby Plaquemines Parish and in doing so removed thirty one place names.[11] Dramatic and subtle changes are presently taking place.[12] Tracing the trajectory of these changes involves diligence, a fearlessness to look at difficulty and a willingness to share the findings, however unsettling they may be.

Ark Hive offers textual contemplation that can be unraveled and parsed over a long duration. It beckons a unhurried focus and calibrated sensitivity toward shifting assemblages that open up an understanding of the complexity of ongoingness of sentient consciousness. Listening for silences, for the voices that have been silenced Reed represents the occlusions with variegated form and tone opening up for representation the meanings that that had been foreclosed. Innumerable voices proliferate their orientations, unspool the logics of the map and points of reference grow into another. Responsive to the range of contingencies that terrestrial life involves this text is a breathing chronicle of interwoven tangibility--relevancy. Living with edges and uncertainty Marthe demonstrates becoming fluid to find open possibility, extending generously in all ways human animals are capable of through acts of language and experientially as citizen-activist-teacher-lover-mother-friend-witness.

---

11   https://geog.ucsb.edu/louisianas-coastal-landmarks-are-being-wiped-off-the-map/#

12   Elizabeth Rush, *Rising: Dispatches From the New American Shore*, Milkweed Editions, 2018, p. 28

EDITOR's NOTE : On *ARK HIVE* After Marthe
ELÆ / LYNNE DESILVA-JOHNSON

When Marthe passed in the Spring of 2018, we had only recently accepted ARK HIVE for the 2019 catalog. She had been incredibly enthusiastic about the new "cohort" model, and even though we'd only just worked together towards this project for short time, she generously offered getting OS books to the NOLA Poetry Festival, which I had been scheduled to attend and perform at, but wouldn't be able to attend.

Marthe's last email to me, on April 9th, gave instructions on how to ship our books to Pack Rat in New Orleans, where, she wrote, she would pick them up along Black Radish titles. She died the following day—and the 2018 NOLA festival would become, for many, a place to celebrate Marthe's life and mourn her loss.

In the months that followed, I learned from countless friends and colleagues that this type of quick kindness and generosity was a hallmark of Marthe's way of being in the world—indeed, even to those she didn't know well... like me, in this case.

It had already been clear when I accepted ARK HIVE for publication, especially in conversation with Brenda Iijima (who originally sent me a hard copy for consideration perhaps a year before its acceptance) that this work was a magnum opus of a human with deep care, deep awareness, boundless curiousity, and a desire to seek, document, archive, and represent both environs and humans alike with honor, humility, and respect.

It has been a gift to have the opportunity to work on this book and in celebrating both its publication and Marthe's work with the poetry and publishing community and especially with her community. I am indebted to Michael Kalish, Lori Anderson Moseman, Brenda Iijima, Henk Rossouw, Amish Trivedi at Jacket 2, Kristina Marie Darling at Tupelo Quarterly, and so many others for supporting this project though ongoing dialogue, collaboration, organizing, and by publishing excerpts of the work.

My last note is an editorial one. I must add here that Marthe and I did not get a chance to work through any edits of this work before her passing, and so the work you see has been unaltered and unedited from the version I received in respect for her not having the opportunity to engage with that process. That said, there is a lot of difficult material here, and in a handful of cases, short pieces or quotations have been removed that Marthe did not get a chance to work through edits on with me that I felt would have needed to be altered to be publication ready. I made this decision aided by a number of external sensitivity readers, and in conversation with others central to the project. I wish I had had a chance to work through this with Marthe, but I trust that as editor and publisher alike, she would respect and honor this difficult choice, as she did everything in her path.

ABOUT THE AUTHOR : IN MEMORIAM

ARK HIVE is Marthe Reed's sixth book, published after her sudden passing in April 2018. Her previous titles were: *Nights Reading* (Lavender Ink, 2014); *Pleth*, with j/j hastain (Unlikely Books, 2013); *(em)bodied bliss* (Moria Books, 2013); *Gaze* (Black Radish Books, 2010); and *Tender Box, A Wunderkammer* (Lavender Ink, 2007). Marthe was also the author of six chapbooks, including the collaborative chapbook *thrown*, text by j/j hastain with Reed's collages, which won the 2013 Smoking Glue Gun contest (2016). Her poetry was published in *BAX2014, New American Writing, Golden Handcuffs Review, Entropy, New Orleans Review, Jacket2, Fairy Tale Review, Exquisite Corpse, The Volta,* and *The Offending Adam*, among others. Her poetry reviews have appeared in *Jacket2, Galatea Ressurrects, Openned, Cut Bank, New Pages, The Rumpus* and *Rain Taxi*. She was the co-publisher and managing editor for Black Radish Books.

ABOUT THE OS : WHY PRINT / DOCUMENT?

The Operating System uses the language "print document" to differentiate from the book-object as part of our mission to distinguish the act of documentation-in-book-FORM from the act of publishing as a backwards-facing replication of the book's agentive *role* as it may have appeared the last several centuries of its history. Ultimately, I approach the book as TECHNOLOGY: one of a variety of printed documents (in this case, bound) that humans have invented and in turn used to archive and disseminate ideas, beliefs, stories, and other evidence of production.

Ownership and use of printing presses and access to (or restriction of printed materials) has long been a site of struggle, related in many ways to revolutionary activity and the fight for civil rights and free speech all over the world. While (in many countries) the contemporary quotidian landscape has indeed drastically shifted in its access to platforms for sharing information and in the widespread ability to "publish" digitally, even with extremely limited resources, the importance of publication on physical media has not diminished. In fact, this may be the most critical time in recent history for activist groups, artists, and others to insist upon learning, establishing, and encouraging personal and community documentation practices. Hear me out.

With The OS's print endeavors I wanted to open up a conversation about this: the ultimately radical, transgressive act of creating PRINT /DOCUMENTATION in the digital age. It's a question of the archive, and of history: who gets to tell the story, and what evidence of our life, our behaviors, our experiences are we leaving behind? We can know little to nothing about the future into which we're leaving an unprecedentedly digital document trail — but we can be assured that publications, government agencies, museums, schools, and other institutional powers that be will continue to leave BOTH a digital and print version of their production for the official record. Will we?

As a (rogue) anthropologist and long time academic, I can easily pull up many accounts about how lives, behaviors, experiences — how THE STORY of a time or place — was pieced together using the deep study of correspondence, notebooks, and other physical documents which are no longer the norm in many lives and practices. As we move our creative behaviors towards digital note taking, and even audio and video, what can we predict about future technology that is in any way assuring that our stories will be accurately told – or told at all? How will we leave these things for the record?

In these documents we say:
WE WERE HERE, WE EXISTED, WE HAVE A DIFFERENT STORY

- Elæ [Lynne DeSilva-Johnson], Founder/Creative Director
THE OPERATING SYSTEM, Brooklyn NY 2018

RECENT & FORTHCOMING FULL LENGTH OS PRINT::DOCUMENTS and PROJECTS, 2018-19

2019

Y - Lori Anderson Moseman
Ark Hive-Marthe Reed
I Made for You a New Machine and All it Does is Hope - Richard Lucyshyn
Illusory Borders-Heidi Reszies
A Year of Misreading the Wildcats - Orchid Tierney
We Are Never The Victims - Timothy DuWhite
Of Color: Poets' Ways of Making | An Anthology of Essays on Transformative Poetics - Amanda Galvan Huynh & Luisa A. Igloria, Editors
The Suitcase Tree - Filip Marinovich
In Corpore Sano: Creative Practice and the Challenged* Body - Elae [Lynne DeSilva-Johnson] and Amanda Glassman, Editors

KIN(D)* TEXTS AND PROJECTS

A Bony Framework for the Tangible Universe-D. Allen
Opera on TV-James Brunton
Hall of Waters-Berry Grass
Transitional Object-Adrian Silbernagel

GLOSSARIUM: UNSILENCED TEXTS AND TRANSLATIONS

Śnienie / Dreaming - Marta Zelwan, (Poland, trans. Victoria Miluch)
Alparegho: Pareil-À-Rien / Alparegho, Like Nothing Else - Hélène Sanguinetti (France, trans. Ann Cefola)
High Tide Of The Eyes - Bijan Elahi (Farsi-English/dual-language) trans. Rebecca Ruth Gould and Kayvan Tahmasebian
In the Drying Shed of Souls: Poetry from Cuba's Generation Zero Katherine Hedeen and Víctor Rodríguez Núñez, translators/editors
Street Gloss - Brent Armendinger with translations for Alejandro Méndez, Mercedes Roffé, Fabián Casas, Diana Bellessi, and Néstor Perlongher (Argentina)
Operation on a Malignant Body - Sergio Loo (Mexico, trans. Will Stockton)
Are There Copper Pipes in Heaven - Katrin Ottarsdóttir (Faroe Islands, trans. Matthew Landrum)

2018

An Absence So Great and Spontaneous It Is Evidence of Light - Anne Gorrick
The Book of Everyday Instruction - Chloë Bass
Executive Orders Vol. II - a collaboration with the Organism for Poetic Research
One More Revolution - Andrea Mazzariello
Chlorosis - Michael Flatt and Derrick Mund
Sussuros a Mi Padre - Erick Sáenz
Abandoners - Lesley Ann Wheeler
Jazzercise is a Language - Gabriel Ojeda-Sague
Born Again - Ivy Johnson
Attendance - Rocío Carlos and Rachel McLeod Kaminer
Singing for Nothing - Wally Swist
Walking Away From Explosions in Slow Motion - Gregory Crosby
Field Guide to Autobiography - Melissa Eleftherion

KIN(D)* TEXTS AND PROJECTS

Sharing Plastic - Blake Neme
The Ways of the Monster - Jay Besemer

GLOSSARIUM: UNSILENCED TEXTS AND TRANSLATIONS

The Book of Sounds - Mehdi Navid (Farsi dual language, trans. Tina Rahimi
Kawsay: The Flame of the Jungle - María Vázquez Valdez
(Mexico, trans. Margaret Randall)
Return Trip / Viaje Al Regreso - Israel Dominguez;
(Cuba, trans. Margaret Randall)

for our full catalog please visit:
https://squareup.com/store/the-operating-system/

*deeply discounted Book of the Month and Chapbook Series subscriptions
are a great way to support the OS's projects and publications!*
sign up at: http://www.theoperatingsystem.org/subscribe-join/

DOC U MENT
/däkyəmənt/

First meant "instruction" or "evidence," whether written or not.

noun - a piece of written, printed, or electronic matter that provides information or evidence or that serves as an official record
verb - record (something) in written, photographic, or other form
synonyms - paper - deed - record - writing - act - instrument

[*Middle English, precept, from Old French, from Latin documentum, example, proof, from docre, to teach; see dek- in Indo-European roots.*]

Who is responsible for the manufacture of value?

Based on what supercilious ontology have we landed in a space where we vie against other creative people in vain pursuit of the fleeting credibilities of the scarcity economy, rather than freely collaborating and sharing openly with each other in ecstatic celebration of MAKING?

While we understand and acknowledge the economic pressures and fear-mongering that threatens to dominate and crush the creative impulse, we also believe that **now more than ever we have the tools to relinquish agency via cooperative means,** fueled by the fires of the Open Source Movement.

Looking out across the invisible vistas of that rhizomatic parallel country we can begin to see our community beyond constraints, in the place where intention meets resilient, proactive, collaborative organization.

Here is a document born of that belief, sown purely of imagination and will.
When we document we assert.
We print to make real, to reify our being there.

When we do so with mindful intention to address our process, to open our work to others, to create beauty in words in space, to respect and acknowledge the strength of the page we now hold physical, a thing in our hand, we remind ourselves that, like Dorothy:
we had the power all along, my dears.

THE PRINT! DOCUMENT SERIES
is a project of
the trouble with bartleby
in collaboration with
the operating system

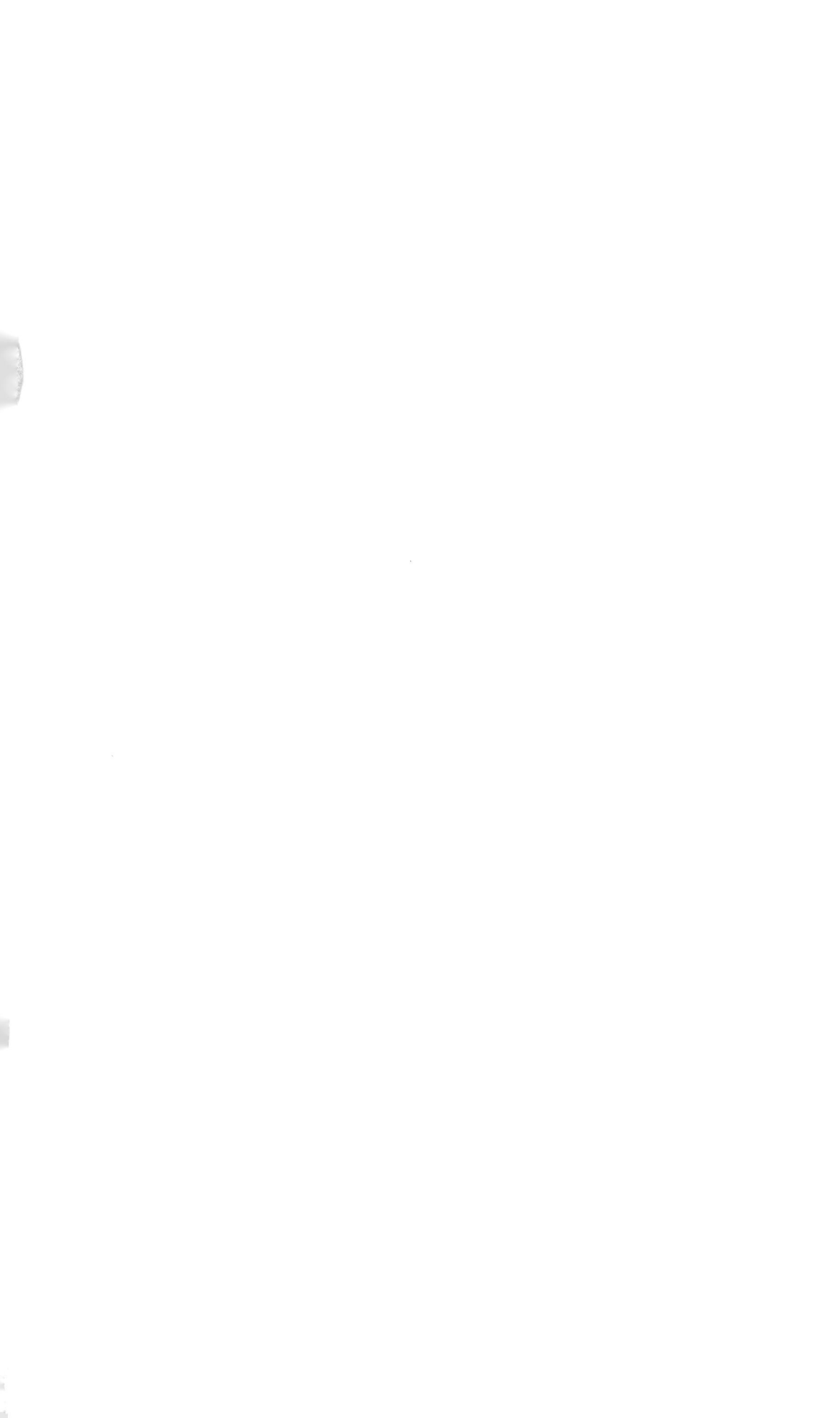

www.ingramcontent.com/pod-product-compliance
Lightning Source LLC
Chambersburg PA
CBHW051333110526
44591CB00026B/2987